The Helicopter Pilot's Manual

Volume 2

The Helicopter Pilot's Manual

Volume 2

Powerplants, Instruments and Hydraulics

Norman Bailey

Airlife
England

This edition published in 1996 by
Airlife Publishing, an imprint of
The Crowood Press Ltd
Ramsbury, Marlborough
Wiltshire SN8 2HR

www.crowood.com

This impression 2005

British Library Cataloguing-in-Publication Data
A catalogue record for this book is available from the British
Library.

ISBN 1 85310 718 2

Typeset by Phoenix Typesetting, Burley-in-Wharfedale

Printed and bound in Great Britain by Livesey Ltd, Shrewsbury

CONTENTS

1

THE HELICOPTER ENGINE

The reciprocating engine is the most widely used powerplant in light helicopters and is designed to specific standards of reliability. It must be capable of sustained high-power output for long periods.

To determine the engine power output, a brake measuring device is attached to the driveshaft. The term used to denote the power developed by the engine is called brake horsepower (bhp).

PRINCIPLE OF OPERATION

The basic principle of operation is the utilisation of air, which when heated by the combustion of fuel expands and in so doing is able to do work. In other words, the engine converts heat energy into mechanical energy.

The main engine components consist of a number of cylinders and pistons with connecting rods to a crankshaft. One end of the connecting rod is attached to the base of the piston and the other to a crankshaft which converts the up-and-down action of the piston into a rotary motion.

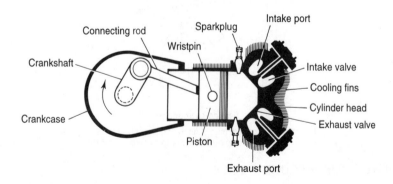

Older types of engine often had the cylinders arranged radially around the crankshaft. Some have the cylinders arranged in one line – the same as in many cars – others have 'V' or 'H' arrangements.

The usual type in many light helicopters has the cylinders arranged in a horizontally–opposed manner.

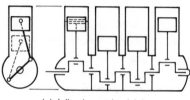

(a) Inline layout (upright)

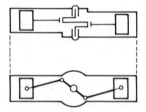

(b) Horizontally opposed

(c) Radial

Engine-cylinder layout

Note that engines with more than two horizontally opposed cylinders
have opposing pistons coupled to a common crankpin.

THE FOUR–STROKE CYCLE

Piston engines operate on the principle of the 'Otto' cycle, named after Nicholas Otto, who built the first successful engine operating by means of pistons moving back and forth inside cylinders. One cycle comprises four strokes of the piston within the cylinder. The four strokes are induction, compression, expansion, exhaust.

Induction Stroke: The fuel/air mixture is induced into the cylinder through an open inlet valve as the piston moves down.

Compression Stroke: The inlet valve closes and the piston begins to move towards the top of the cylinder, compressing the mixture. As the piston is completing the compression stroke, the mixture is ignited by means of a spark plug.

Power Stroke: As the burning mixture expands, it exerts a pressure on the piston and forces it back down the cylinder.

Exhaust Stroke: Just before the completion of the power stroke, the exhaust valve opens and allows the burned gases to escape as the piston rises once more.

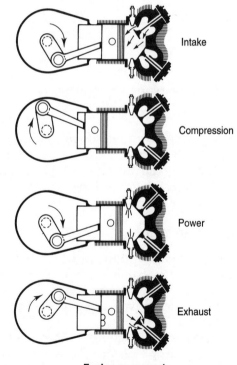

Intake

Compression

Power

Exhaust

Engine power cycle

This cycle continues to repeat itself throughout the period the engine is running. Note that the power stroke occurs once and the crankshaft revolves twice for every four strokes of the piston.

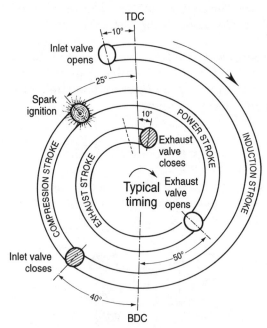

Typical valve timing in the four-stroke cycle

To increase engine power and create more smoothness, more cylinders are added. The power strokes must be timed to occur at different intervals during the revolution of the crankshaft. In a four-cylinder engine, therefore, two revolutions of the crankshaft would receive four impulses of power.

VALVES AND VALVE TIMING

The inlet and exhaust valves, through which the mixture is introduced and exhaust gases expelled, slide back and forth in their guides during engine operation. These valves are normally activated by rocker arms driven directly from a camshaft or via pushrods.

A typical engine speed is 2,900 RPM. Each inlet valve will open once per four strokes of the piston. The same will apply to each exhaust valve. Therefore, the inlet and exhaust valve must open and close once in every two revolutions of the crankshaft. As the camshaft rotates at half engine speed, at 2,900 RPM each valve will have to open and close 1,450 times. (1,450 times per minute = twenty-four times a second!)

As the power developed by the engine is a function of the amount of mixture which can be fed into the cylinder during the intake stroke, it can be seen that the amount of power developed depends on the size of the intake port and the length of time the inlet valve is open.

By opening the inlet valve just before the piston reaches **Top Dead Centre** (TDC), and by not closing it until the piston has gone just past **Bottom Dead Centre** (BDC), maximum time for the intake of the fuel/air mixture is allowed. This is called **valve lead** and **valve lag**.

For a short time at the start of the induction stroke, the burned gases are still being exhausted through the still–open exhaust valve while fresh mixture is passing through the just opened inlet valve. This brief period when both the inlet and exhaust valves are open together is called **valve overlap**.

DETONATION

This is defined as abnormally rapid combustion. If the burning rate of the fuel is too fast, the pressure in the cylinder will build up rapidly and the remaining mixture will detonate.

Continued operation when detonation is present can result in engine damage. Some causes of detonation are low-grade fuel, mixture too lean, high cylinder–head temperature and abruptly opening the throttle when the engine is running at low speeds.

PRE-IGNITION

Pre-ignition is the uncontrolled firing of the mixture in advance of normal spark ignition. It is usually caused by carbon deposits on piston heads, spark plugs and valves.

Pre-ignition can be as destructive as detonation, so proper maintenance and correct operating techniques are necessary to prevent pre-ignition.

IGNITION SYSTEM

The purpose of the ignition system is to provide a high-tension spark to each cylinder in the correct firing order and at a predetermined number of degrees before TDC. This slightly advanced spark is to allow a controlled flame front to start moving through the mixture that has been compressed in the cylinder.

Regardless of the engine type, the basic requirements are the same. The most common is the DUAL IGNITION system, consisting of two high-tension magnetos connected by wiring to two spark plugs in each cylinder. As well as being safer, a more even and efficient combustion results.

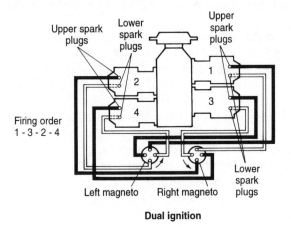

Dual ignition

THE MAGNETOS

The magneto is basically an engine-driven generator which is not connected to the helicopter's main electrical system. It utilises a rotating magnet close to a coil of wire as its source of energy. The rotation of the magnet induces an electrical current to flow in the

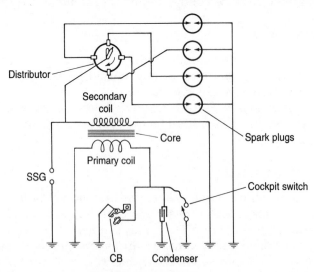

Magneto circuit diagram

coil. Initially the battery is used to activate the magnet via the starter system.

Once the engine has been started, the starter system is disengaged and from then on the battery plays no further part in engine operation. (If the battery switch is turned off the engine will continue to run.)

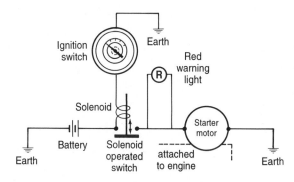

The electric starter system

The high voltage produced by the magneto enables a spark to jump across the spark plug gap and ignite the mixture in the cylinder before the power stroke. The timing of the spark is vital, so, in order for the spark to occur at the right time, the magneto is equipped with breaker points. These points open and close via the action of a small cam connected indirectly to the crankshaft. A distributor assembly feeds the current to the correct cylinder spark plug at the right time in the cycle of piston strokes.

During starting, the starter motor turns the engine relatively slowly, so the electrical current produced by the magneto is weak. To assist in boosting the voltage one of two methods is normally employed:

Impulse Coupler: This is basically a coiled spring attached to an engine accessory driveshaft. As the engine starts to turn, the spring tightens until it becomes fully compressed. It then releases itself and spins the magneto fast enough to develop enough current to produce a spark at the plug.

Vibrator: This depends on current from the battery, which is passed through the magneto's primary coil, building up to a high voltage. When this is released at the proper time it delivers a continuous stream of sparks.

Both of these methods automatically disengage once the engine starts.

IGNITION SWITCHES

The ignition system is controlled through the ignition switches which have four positions: OFF, LEFT, RIGHT, BOTH.

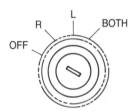

If LEFT is selected, only the left magneto supplies a spark. The engine will run on just one magneto, but not as smoothly as on two. **CAUTION:** One main difference between ignition switches and other electrical switches is that when the ignition switch is turned to OFF, the primary winding of the magneto is earthed so that it no longer supplies power. In other electrical switches the OFF position normally opens the circuit.

FUEL SYSTEMS

The fuel system is made up of two groups of components, the supply system and the induction system. The supply system takes the fuel from the tank and delivers it to the engine. The induction system vaporises the fuel, mixes it with air in the correct ratio and delivers it into the combustion chamber.

Supply System

The supply system consists of one or more fuel tanks, a strainer to remove sediments and water, a fuel quantity gauge, a fuel shut-off valve and a fuel line to the engine.

The most common supply system in a helicopter is the gravity-feed type, in which the fuel tank(s) are mounted above the level of the engine. A mechanical pump is used to provide a continuous supply of fuel from the tank to the engine. For safety reasons, engine-driven fuel pumps are normally designed to be capable of supplying more fuel than the engine requires. Therefore, a fuel pressure relief valve is incorporated in the system to permit unused fuel to return to the inlet side of the pump, or alternatively directly to the fuel tank.

As a safety precaution against mechanical pump failure, a separate electrical boost pump is also fitted. This electrical pump will also be needed to prime the system before engine starting.

The fuel tank contains a filler neck and fuel cap, a quantity transmitter, a drain tap and outlet fittings. The top of each tank is vented to outside air so that atmospheric pressure can be maintained in the tank as fuel is used up. If the vent becomes blocked for any reason, a reduced pressure will be created in the area above the head of fuel and will reduce the normal rate of fuel flow. Airworthiness requirements demand that the fuel caps or the areas adjacent to them are clearly marked with the correct fuel grade and tank capacity.

A fuel strainer is located at the lowest point in the fuel system. Since water is heavier than fuel, any water in the fuel will collect at this point. It can then be drained off through the fuel strainer drain valve. A filter element in the strainer traps any impurities contained in the fuel. A small amount of fuel should be drained from the strainer during each pre-flight inspection to check for water contamination.

Fuel Induction Systems
Piston-engined helicopters are equipped with either a CARBURETTOR or FUEL INJECTOR induction system.

Carburettor: In order that the fuel can ignite, it needs an adequate supply of oxygen. This is achieved by mixing the fuel with air at a

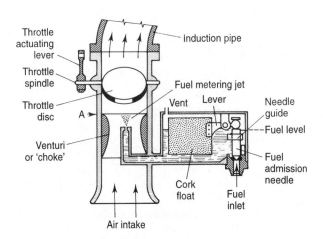

A simple carburettor

ratio that enables it to burn properly within the cylinders. The chemically correct ratio is fifteen parts of air to one part of fuel.

On helicopter engines a carburettor is used to meter the airflow through the induction system and regulate the amount of fuel discharged into the induction airstream. It uses the venturi principle inside a cylinder, which causes a drop in pressure and draws fuel into the airstream. The amount of air is controlled by a butterfly valve connected to the throttle. Fuel jets are positioned in the venturi to meter the correct amount of fuel. The size and shape of the venturi depends on the size of the engine. When the carburettor is positioned so that the air passes upwards through it to the cylinders, it is known as an updraught carburettor. The converse of this is a downdraught carburettor.

Initially, fuel enters the carburettor at the float valve and flows into the float chamber until it reaches a certain level. When the float rises to a predetermined height it shuts off the float valve. No additional fuel is allowed to enter until fuel is used by the engine. The float chamber is vented so that pressure will not build up in the chamber as altitude increases.

On its way to the engine the outside air first passes through an air filter located at the carburettor air intake. After the air is filtered, it passes through a venturi in the carburettor. This venturi creates a low–pressure area and, with the float chamber vented to atmosphere, fuel is forced to flow from the float chamber through the main

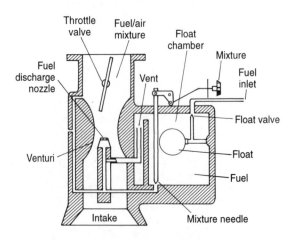

Carburettor components

jet and mixes with air flowing in from outside. A mixture control located on the instrument panel regulates the amount of fuel that passes through the main jet and, therefore, fuel consumption.

If the fuel/air mixture is too lean, rough engine operation, back-firing, detonation, overheating and loss of engine power may occur. If the mixture is too rich, rough engine operation and an apprecia-ble loss of power may also occur. Excessive fuel will cause lower than normal temperatures in the combustion chamber. Since spark plugs need sufficient heat to burn any excess carbon and lead, the plugs may become fouled if the mixture is too rich.

Carburettors are normally calibrated for sea-level operation, which means that the correct mixture will be obtained at sea level with the mixture control set at full rich. As altitude increases, the air density decreases, which means that the weight of air entering the carburettor decreases although the volume remains the same. The amount of fuel entering the carburettor depends on the volume and *not* on the weight of air. Therefore, as altitude increases, the amount of fuel entering the carburettor remains approximately the same for any given throttle setting if the position of the mixture control remains unchanged. Since the same amount (weight) of fuel is entering the carburettor, but a lesser amount of air, the fuel/air mixture becomes richer with increased altitude.

To maintain the correct fuel/air ratio, the pilot must be able to adjust the amount of fuel mixed with the incoming air as altitude increases. This is accomplished by leaning the mixture.

Carburettor Icing

Carburettor icing can cause loss of power or even engine stoppage during flight. The vaporisation of fuel combined with the expansion of air passing through the carburettor causes a sudden cooling of the mixture.

The temperature of the air may drop by as much as 40°C (104°F). Any water vapour present in the air is condensed by this cooling and, if the temperature in the carburettor reaches 0°C (32°F) or below, the moisture is deposited as frost or ice inside the carburet-tor passages. Even a slight accumulation will reduce power and may even lead to engine stoppage, particularly if the throttle is partly or fully closed.

Carburettor icing is still possible in temperatures as high as 40°C (104°F) and humidity as low as 50%. However, it is most likely in temperatures below 20°C (68°F) and with relative humidity above 80%. As the temperature decreases towards 0°C (32°F) or, as the humidity increases, the chance of carburettor icing increases.

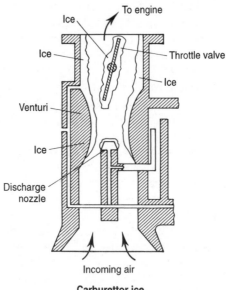

Carburettor ice

Since the throttle is constantly being adjusted to maintain engine RPM the advent of carburettor icing would be difficult to detect. Therefore helicopters equipped with carburettors have a carburettor heat system to safeguard against ice formation. A heater muff around the engine exhaust and a control valve allow the pilot to select unheated outside air, hot air from the intake air heater or a mixture of both. A carburettor air temperature gauge on the instrument panel permits the air intake to be regulated within a temperature range not conducive to the formation of carburettor ice.

Fuel Injection System
Fuel injection eliminates the problem of carburettor ice and the need for a carburettor heat system. Fuel Injection system: This consists of an engine-driven pump, fuel injector unit, flow divider, fuel lines and injector nozzles. An electric boost pump is used for priming the system before starting and to supply pressure in case of mechanical pump failure.

The injector unit (sometimes called the servo control), takes fuel under pressure from the engine-driven pump. Airflow from the engine induction system is measured and fuel is metered in proportion to airflow. It then passes to the flow divider for distribution through individual lines to each cylinder injector. Injector nozzles in each cylinder spray the fuel into the manifold where it mixes with air as it is drawn into the cylinder through the intake valve. The

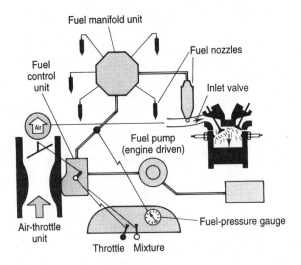

Fuel manifold unit

Fuel nozzles

Fuel control unit

Inlet valve

Air

Fuel pump (engine driven)

Fuel-pressure gauge

Air-throttle unit

Throttle   Mixture

A fuel injection system

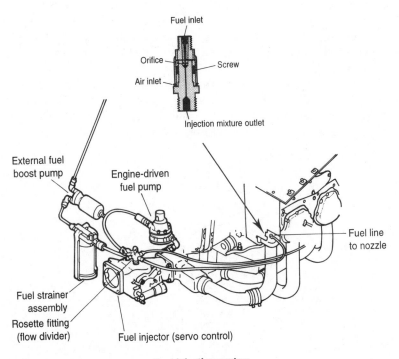

Fuel inlet

Orifice

Screw

Air inlet

Injection mixture outlet

External fuel boost pump

Engine-driven fuel pump

Fuel line to nozzle

Fuel strainer assembly

Rosette fitting (flow divider)

Fuel injector (servo control)

Fuel injection system

mixture is then ignited at the top of the compression stroke of the piston.

The servo control is the heart of the system. It measures the air-flow as demanded by the throttle setting and meters fuel precisely under all conditions of power and air density. The result is a correct fuel/air mixture for all operating conditions.

The fuel flow divider directs fuel evenly to each cylinder. It is injected into the air induction manifold by the injector nozzles. The nozzles atomise the fuel as it enters the manifold to assist in vapor-isation. Mixing the fuel and air at this point helps to ensure more even fuel distribution in the cylinders and better vaporisation. This in turn promotes more efficient use of the fuel.

TURBOCHARGING

When a piston engine is operated at higher density altitudes, efficiency diminishes as a result of a smaller volume of airflow being processed. Therefore, a turbocharger may be added to the engine to compress air before it is injected into the cylinders.

The difference between a turbocharger and a supercharger is that the former is powered by exhaust gases, while the latter is mechanically driven from the crankshaft. Using exhaust gases to power the turbocharger has two main advantages: it is a free power source and the unit can be of lighter and more compact construction.

There are two sections to the turbocharger, the turbine and the compressor. Exhaust gases leaving the engine are directed on to the turbine, setting it spinning before exiting through the exhaust pipe. The turbine is connected by a shaft to the compressor. As the

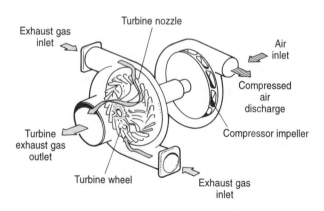

compressor rotates it draws in intake air, compresses it and delivers it to the cylinders. This compression increases air density, so that a helicopter engine can operate at low-density altitudes and still produce the same amount of power as it would at sea level.

To avoid damage to the engine there has to be some method of limiting this boosted pressure. This is usually achieved by means of a safety valve called a wastegate. Simply, this is just a spring-loaded valve that is fitted on to the exhaust manifold upstream of the turbine. A line is then tapped into the inlet manifold downstream of the compressor and connected to the wastegate. At maximum allowed pressure the wastegate opens and allows the exhaust gas to bypass the turbine.

Because turbochargers operate at high temperatures and rotate at very high revolutions, it is vital that their shaft bearings are adequately supplied with engine oil. To solve the problem of the oil breaking down under these operating conditions, it is extremely important to carry out the engine run-down and cooling procedures as laid down by the manufacturer.

AVIATION FUEL

Aviation gasoline, (Avgas), consists almost entirely of hydrocarbons, that is, compounds composed of hydrogen and carbon. The volatility of a fuel (its tendency to vaporise) is controlled during manufacture.

If fuel vaporises too readily it can cause vapour in the fuel lines and so decrease the rate of fuel flow. If the fuel does not vaporise readily it can cause difficult engine starting, uneven fuel distribution to the cylinder and retarded engine acceleration.

Helicopter engines vary widely in the power they can produce and it is therefore necessary to produce varying grades of aviation fuel. These different grades are identified by a numerical code system. To assist in identification, all aviation gasoline contains a coloured dye and the allocation of different colours to different fuel grades is standardised throughout the world; for example Avgas, grade 100LL (Low Lead) is coloured blue.

Using aviation fuel rated higher that that specified does not improve engine operation, but neither is it considered harmful if only used for a short period of time. Using a lower grade of fuel is definitely harmful under any circumstances, because it may cause loss of power, excessive heat, burned spark plugs, burned valves and detonation. If the correct grade of fuel required is not available, the next *higher* grade should be used. *Never* use a *lower* grade.

Car petrol is not controlled during manufacture to the same tolerances as aviation fuel. Therefore, except when permitted by the Airworthiness Division of the Civil Aviation Authority, car petrol should *not* be used in helicopter engines.

ENGINE COOLING

The burning of fuel within the cylinders produces intense heat. Much of this engine heat is expelled with the escaping gases or exhaust but to keep modern helicopter engines cooled, outside air must circulate around the cylinders.

There are four main reasons why excessive heat should be avoided:

a) it weakens engine components and shortens engine life
b) it reduces the efficiency of the lubricating system
c) it can cause detonation to occur
d) it affects the behaviour of the combustion of the mixture

The engine is built with thin metal fins projecting from the cylinder walls. Air is circulated over the engine and oil cooler by means of an engine-driven cooling fan mounted in a shroud. Cylinder baffles direct the air evenly over the cooling fins and are designed to obtain maximum cooling efficiency. This even distribution of the airflow helps to prevent local hotspots in any one cylinder, or more than one cylinder, from becoming much hotter than the rest. A cylinder-head temperature gauge is fitted on the instrument panel to allow the pilot to monitor engine temperature whenever the engine is running.

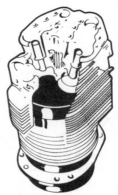

Cooling fins

ENGINE LUBRICATION

Engine lubrication is necessary to reduce friction and therefore wear between the moving parts. In addition, as the oil is circulated through the engine it absorbs heat and thereby assists in engine cooling. During its circulation, oil also collects dirt introduced into the engine from the atmosphere and carbon particles produced by combustion. These are all collected by the oil filter, reducing abrasive wear on the internal parts.

Apart from absorbing foreign matter, oil undergoes two chemical changes during use. Firstly, oxidation occurs owing to contamination from corrosive lead salts produced during combustion. Secondly, water vapour condenses inside the engine as the oil cools after the engine has stopped. These effects cannot be filtered out and therefore it is important to adhere to the oil change periods specified in the maintenance schedule.

Aviation oils are classified numerically to indicate the degree of viscosity. A high-viscosity oil flows slowly and a low-viscosity oil flows freely. It is important that the correct grade of oil, as recommended in the flight manual, is used throughout the engine's life.

Engine lubrication systems are either a **wet sump** or a **dry sump** type. A wet sump stores the oil as an integral part of the engine casing and the components are lubricated by a pressure pump or simply by splash lubrication. The dry sump system has a separate oil tank, and passes oil to the engine via a pressure pump. After lubrication, the oil is returned to the tank by a separate scavenge pump.

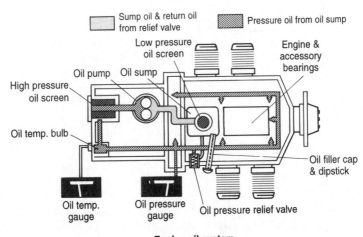

Engine oil system

Two gauges on the instrument panel show engine oil temperature and engine oil pressure. The oil temperature indicated is usually the temperature of the oil as it leaves the oil cooler. The oil pressure shown is the pressure at which the oil enters the engine from the oil pump.

HYDRAULIC SYSTEMS

The hydraulic systems used in light helicopters are mainly to assist in the operation of flying controls. Although there are various types of systems, they all utilise the basic property of incompressibility of liquids.

If a can of water is full to the top, no more water can be added without it spilling over. This is because liquid will not compress. The liquid used in hydraulic systems is oil. If you apply a force on top of the oil, that force is transmitted down to the bottom because the oil will not compress. If a force of one pound per square inch is applied to the top, then a force of one pound per square inch will be felt at the bottom. A further advantage of this property of liquids lies in the fact that, if the bottom of the can is wider than the top, the pressure on the bottom would still be one pound per square inch. In this way a small pressure at the narrow end of the system can produce a large pressure at the wider end.

Normally, a piston is fitted in a small cylinder to exert pressure on fluid in a connecting pipe to a larger cylinder, also fitted with a piston. The small cylinder is called the **master cylinder** and the larger one the **actuating cylinder**.

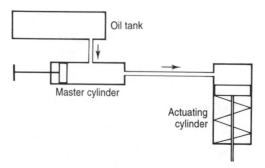

To prevent fluid rushing backwards into the master cylinder, a non-return valve (NRV) is fitted between the master and actuating cylinders. The fluid in the system is now held under pressure.

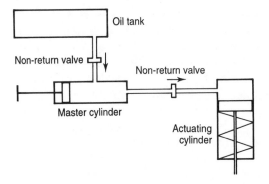

In order that the pressure can be released to allow the piston to move the other way, a return line must be introduced, together with a selector valve.

To operate the system at working pressure, a power pump is included and a pressure relief valve (PRV) incorporated.

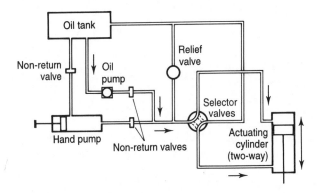

All hydraulic fluids are inflammable and, if there is any leakage into the cabin, windows must be opened to allow the fumes to escape.

ELECTRICAL SYSTEMS

All light helicopters are equipped with either a 14V or 28V direct current, negative earth, electrical system powered by an engine-driven generator or alternator. A battery serves as a standby power source in case the generator or alternator malfunctions and also powers the starter and other electrical equipment when the engine is not running.

Alternators have the advantage over generators of being more efficient at low engine RPM, lighter in weight and usually of costing less to maintain. Operation of the alternator is controlled by a switch on the instrument panel. When the alternator switch is OFF and the battery switch is ON, electrical equipment is powered by the battery except for the ignition system, which receives its power from the magnetos. The alternator generates alternating current which is rectified, by diodes inside the alternator, to direct current. The diodes also prevent the battery from discharging through the alternator when the output voltage is low. The correct output voltage from the alternator is maintained by the voltage regulator.

The ammeter indicates whether or not the battery is being charged. When the needle is pointing to the right side (+), electrical energy is flowing into the battery. When the needle is deflected to the left side (–), more electrical energy is being used than is being replaced by the generating system.

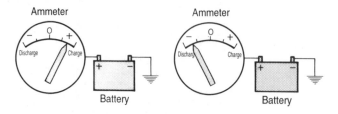

As a precaution against damaging electrical equipment through overloading, each circuit is normally provided with a fuse or circuit breaker.

If an overload occurs, the affected circuit breaker pops out and power is removed from the circuit. The circuit breaker can be reset by pressing it back in to restore power to the circuit, but if it pops out a second time an electrical problem is indicated. In this case the circuit should remain unpowered until the fault can be repaired.

VACUUM SYSTEMS

Electricity is universally used on all modern helicopters to operate gyroscopic instruments. Vacuum systems are discussed here in general to increase pilot background knowledge.

All gyro instruments operated by the vacuum system are driven by air pressure differential. An engine-driven suction pump creates a partial vacuum in the system which causes air to rush in. This airflow is directed so as to cause the gyro to spin at a very high speed. The air is then exhausted to atmosphere through the pump. The degree of vacuum normally required to drive the gyros is between 3.5 and 5.5 in. of mercury and this is controlled by a vacuum relief valve located in the supply line. A vacuum pressure gauge is usually mounted on the instrument panel to monitor the difference, in inches of mercury, between the pressure at the central filter and at the pressure relief valve. A zero reading indicates that either the vacuum pump or the instrument itself has failed.

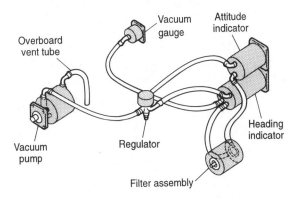

The main components of the vacuum system are:

Oil Recuperator: This is a metal box containing a filter in which the lubricating and cooling oil from the pump is separated. The latest types of suction pumps are self-lubricating in which case an oil recuperator is not required.

Vacuum Regulator: This is basically a pressure relief valve in reverse which is adjusted to permit the required suction. Any build-up beyond this is regulated by allowing atmospheric pressure to enter the system.

Filter System: Air filters are used to prevent foreign matter from entering the system and damaging the gyro bearings. When the filters become dirty the airflow through the system is reduced, resulting in a lower reading on the vacuum gauge.

2

AIRWORTHINESS

THE CERTIFICATE OF AIRWORTHINESS

With few exceptions all helicopters must be issued with a Certificate of Airworthiness (C of A), which covers a specified time period and has to be in force for the helicopter to fly.

Because helicopters are able to operate for different purposes, Cs of A are issued in specific categories:

Transport Category (Passenger)	Can be used for any purpose.
Transport Category (Cargo)	Any purpose other than the transport of passengers.
Aerial Work Category	For aerial work only.
Private Category	Any purpose other than Public Transport or Aerial Work.
Special Category	Any purpose other than Public Transport, specified in the certificate, but not including the carriage of passengers unless expressly permitted.

Before issuing or renewing a C of A, the Civil Aviation Authority (CAA) must be satisfied that the helicopter is fit to fly and airworthy in all respects. The results of maintenance inspections and any flight tests will also be assessed in accordance with the requirements laid down in the British Civil Airworthiness Requirements (BCARs).

The helicopter's flight manual is incorporated with the C of A. This means that the pilot will have to abide by the operating limitations laid down in the flight manual if the validity of the C of A is to be maintained. If the operating limitations are not complied with, the C of A will automatically be invalidated and any warranty in force or insurance policy put at risk. The helicopter must not be flown after the expiry date unless an exemption has been granted by the CAA.

HELICOPTER LOGBOOKS

In order to maintain a record of any repairs, changes or modifications to the helicopter and replacement of lifed components, the following records must be kept:

a) Aircraft logbook

b) Engine logbook

c) Component history cards

It is the operator's responsibility to ensure that the logbooks are kept up to date in respect of the flight times completed. A twin-engined helicopter must keep a separate logbook for each engine. These records must be preserved by the owner for two years after the helicopter or engine, as the case may be, has been destroyed or permanently withdrawn from use.

THE MAINTENANCE SCHEDULE

Most light helicopters are maintained under the CAA Light Aircraft Maintenance Schedule – Rotary Wing (LAMS/H). This schedule is available for helicopters which have a maximum all-up weight not exceeding 2,730 kg and it lists the maintenance cycle as follows:

Public Transport and Aerial Work Category
Check A: prior to first flight of the day.
50-hour Check: not exceeding fifty flying hours or sixty-two days, whichever is the sooner.
100-hour Check: not exceeding 100 flying hours.
Annual Check: not exceeding twelve months.

Private Category
Check A: prior to first flight of the day.
50-hour Check: not exceeding fifty flying hours.
100-hour Check: not exceeding 100 flying hours.
Annual Check: not exceeding twelve months.

CERTIFICATE OF RELEASE TO SERVICE

Whenever work has been completed involving overhaul, repair, replacement, modification, scheduled or mandatory inspection, a Certificate of Release to Service must be issued.

CERTIFICATE OF MAINTENANCE REVIEW

These are required only for helicopters certificated in the Public Transport and Aerial Work categories. The Certificate of Maintenance Review shall be certificated at each annual inspection by the licensed engineer carrying out the work.

PILOT'S RESPONSIBILITY

It is the pilot's responsibility to check whether the helicopter's documentation and serviceability is satisfactory before each flight. He is also responsible for entering any unserviceability of the helicopter and its components in the technical log, or its equivalent, immediately after the flight.

PILOT MAINTENANCE

Before 1 April 1971, legislation required any repair or replacement of components which are necessary for airworthiness, even of a minor nature, to be carried out under the supervision of a licensed engineer.

As a result of consultation it has been decided that this procedure was unnecessarily restrictive and that pilots licensed on type should be allowed to carry out minor repairs, replacements and lubrication on helicopters not exceeding 2,730kg (6,000 lb) maximum total weight and used for purposes *other than Public Transport.*

At the time of writing this manual, such rectification work consisted of the following:
a) replacement of landing gear tyres, landing skids or skid shoes
b) replacement of elastic shock absorber cord units on landing gear where special tools are not required
c) replacement of defective safety wiring or split pins, excluding those in engine, transmission, flight control and rotor systems
d) patch repairs to fabric not requiring rib stitching or the removal of structural parts or control surfaces, if the repairs do not cover up structural damage and do not include repairs to rotor blades
e) repairs to upholstery and decorative furnishing of the cabin or cockpit interior when repair does not require dismantling of any structure or operating system or interfere with an operating system or affect the structure of the helicopter
f) repairs not requiring welding to fairings, non-structural cover plates and cowlings
g) replacement of side windows where that work does not interfere with the structure or with any operating system
h) replacement of safety belts or safety harness
i) replacement of seats or seat parts not involving dismantling of any structure or of any operating system

j)   replacement of bulbs, reflectors, glasses, lenses or lights
k)   replacement of any cowling not requiring removal of the propeller, rotors or disconnection of engine or flight controls
l)   replacement of unserviceable sparking plugs
m) replacement of batteries
n)   replacement of wings and tail surfaces and controls, the attachments of which are designed to provide for assembly immediately before such flight and dismantling after each flight
o)   replacement of main rotor blades that are designed for removal where special tools are not required
p)   replacement of generator, alternator and fan belts designed where special tools are not required

In addition to the above, pilots are permitted to carry out normal cleaning and lubrication procedures such as:

a)   cleaning and greasing of landing gear wheel bearings
b)   lubrication not requiring disassembly other than the removal of non-structural items such as cover plates, cowlings and fairings
c)   applying preservative or protective material to components where disassembly of any primary structure or operating system is not involved and where such coating is not proscribed or not contrary to good practice
d)   cleaning fuel filters

NOTE: In performing maintenance, pilots should exercise the utmost discretion and not attempt any work which requires special technical knowledge or skill beyond their ability or facilities.

DUPLICATE INSPECTION

Any adjustments that are made to either the flight controls and/or engine controls of a helicopter are normally required to be checked by two licensed engineers before it is considered to be airworthy again. BCARs state, however, that should a minor adjustment be necessary while the helicopter is away from base, the second part of the duplicate inspection may be completed by a pilot who is licenced on the helicopter type.

QUESTIONS AND ANSWERS

1.   During the normal operating cycle of a piston engine, ignition occurs:
     A) at top dead centre
     B) After top dead centre
     C) before top dead centre

2. Prolonged engine operation at maximum power is not recommended because of:
   A) the tendency for power to 'fall off' after the time limit has been exceeded
   B) the long-term effects of engine wear
   C) the dangers of exceeding maximum oil pressure

3. In the event of an air intake fire during engine start, the engine should be:
   A) kept turning while the mixture is selected to Idle Cut Off and the throttle selected Open
   B) stopped immediately
   C) kept turning while the fire extinguisher is discharged into the air intake

4. After starting a cold engine, if the oil pressure gauge does not indicate within approximately thirty seconds:
   A) the helicopter may be hover-taxied to the departure point and the oil pressure rechecked
   B) this may be ignored if the oil temperature is still low and the oil level had been checked before start-up
   C) the engine must be stopped immediately

5. The cycle of operations of a helicopter piston engine takes place in the following order:
   A) induction, compression, exhaust, power
   B) induction, compression, power, exhaust
   C) induction, power, compression, exhaust

6. The ignition switch directly controls:
   A) the supply of current to the spark plugs
   B) the battery supply to the magneto primary windings
   C) the earthing of the magneto primary windings

7. When a magneto is switched off, the primary winding:
   A) is earthed through the switch
   B) is isolated from earth
   C) is isolated from the battery power

8. The high-tension supply for the spark plugs is derived from the:
   A) battery and transformed by the magneto
   B) magneto's self-contained generation and distribution system
   C) battery during starting and the magneto once the engine is running

9. When a fuel-priming pump is used before starting, the fuel is normally delivered directly to the:
   A) combustion chamber
   B) induction manifold or inlet valve port

C) carburettor float chamber

10. Use of the mixture control in the carburettor:
    A) adjusts the fuel flow to the main jet
    B) alters the airflow through the venturi
    C) controls the fuel flow by adjusting the float valve

11. Under normal running conditions, ignition of fuel and air mixture in the engine cylinder takes place:
    A) at the beginning of the exhaust stroke
    B) just after the start of the power stroke
    C) just before the end of the compression stroke

12. The oil system of a helicopter engine:
    A) lubricates the moving parts and assists in cooling the engine
    B) lubricates the moving parts but does not assist cooling
    C) improves combustion efficiency

13. Prolonged ground running at idling speed will reduce subsequent engine efficiency because:
    A) the engine will have cooled below operational levels
    B) of overheating the valves
    C) of carbon build-up on the spark plugs

14. It is important to carry out regular checks for water in the fuel system, since if water is present it will cause:
    A) carburettor venturi icing
    B) the fuel to freeze
    C) contamination of the fuel system resulting in loss of engine power

15. Carburettor icing may be encountered:
    A) in air temperatures up to +25°C
    B) in air temperatures below 0°C only
    C) in air temperatures below +10°C only

16. An ignition switch in the OFF position:
    A) directly disconnects the high-voltage supply to the spark plugs
    B) disconnects the battery supply from the magneto
    C) connects the magneto circuit to earth

17. A bus bar is:
    A) a device facilitating the operation of two or more switches together
    B) the non-moving part of a moving coil instrument
    C) a distribution point for electrical power

18. The Certificate of Airworthiness:
    A) expires only on removal of the helicopter from the British register
    B) is valid indefinitely providing the helicopter is maintained

in accordance with the requirements specified on the C of A document

C) expires on the date stated on the C of A document

19. A helicopter maintained to the Light Aircraft Maintenance Schedule within the Private Category requires a Check A:
    A) every day and it must be carried out by a licensed engineer
    B) prior to the first flight of the day and carried out to the satisfaction of the pilot
    C) before each flight and carried out to the satisfaction of the owner

20. A pilot can sign the second part of a duplicate inspection for a control system provided he has:
    A) an instructor's rating and that the trim system is not disturbed
    B) 100 hours' experience and a maintenance manual; also the subsequent flight must be back to base only
    C) a pilot's licence valid for the type and that the adjustment is of a minor nature.

ANSWERS

1. C	11. C
2. B	12. A
3. A	13. C
4. C	14. C
5. B	15. A
6. C	16. C
7. A	17. C
8. B	18. C
9. B	19. B
10. A	20. C

3

FLIGHT INSTRUMENTS

Although early helicopters had very limited instrumentation, the modern types can be extremely well equipped. The flight instruments are those which are used in controlling the helicopter and can be divided into two groups:

a) Pressure-operated Instruments (altimeter, airspeed indicator and vertical speed indicator)

b) Gyroscopic Instruments (artificial horizon, directional heading indicator and turn/slip indicator)

PRESSURE-OPERATED INSTRUMENTS

The pitot-static system is the means of supplying air pressure to the pressure-operated instruments. Two types of pressure are required, static pressure and dynamic pressure. All three instruments require static pressure. In addition, the airspeed indicator also requires dynamic pressure.

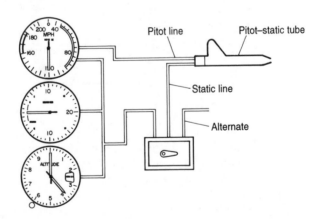

Pressure Error: An error known as the pressure error can develop as a result of disturbances in airflow around the pitot head. The size of the error will depend on:

a) the position of the pitot tube

b) the attitude of the helicopter

c) airspeed

Most of the errors result from variations in the local static pressure caused by the airflow over the static ports. This error is minimised when the static ports are positioned on the side of the fuselage where the truest static pressure can be found.

The Altimeter

Pressure altimeters are simply aneroid barometers graduated to indicate height instead of pressure above a preselected pressure datum. They operate on the principle that air pressure decreases with height.

A simple altimeter consists of a partially evacuated capsule mounted inside an airtight case. The case is fed with static pressure from the helicopter's static port. As the helicopter climbs, pressure in the case falls and allows a spring to pull against the capsule. Conversely, a decrease in height compresses the capsule. This movement is magnified and transmitted to a pointer moving over a dial on the face of the instrument. As the local atmospheric pressure is constantly changing, it is necessary to set the altimeter before take-off.

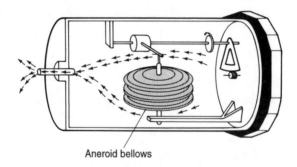

Aneroid bellows

A simple altimeter is designed for more accurate height measurement. Although the principle of operation is the same, it uses two or more evacuated capsules for greater sensitivity and a millibar subscale.

Altimeters are calibrated on the assumption that the International Standard Atmosphere will apply. This assumes that the sea-level pressure is 1013.2 millibars and that the temperature is 15°C, lapsing at a rate of 1.98°C per thousand feet up to 36,000 feet. The temperature lapse rate has a direct bearing on the relationship between height and pressure. Therefore, if the actual temperature lapse rate is very different from standard, the altimeter readings will be inaccurate.

Errors

Errors inherent in the instrument and installation are:

a) Instrument Error
b) Pressure Error
c) Time Lag
d) Hysteresis Error

Errors due to variations in the atmosphere are:

e) Barometric Error
f) Temperature Error

Instrument Error: Since capsule movements have to be magnified it is impossible to avoid completely the effect of irregularities in the mechanism. On a well-made instrument these should be negligible.

Pressure Error: Inherent in any aircraft pressure system. It should be insignificant in a helicopter fitted with static ports.

Time Lag: Since the response of the capsule and linkage is not instantaneous, the altimeter lags whenever height is changed rapidly.

Hysteresis Error: A capsule under stress is not perfectly elastic. Its deflection for a given change of pressure will vary slightly, depending on whether the pressure is increasing or decreasing.

Barometric Error: The difference between the actual sea-level pressure and standard pressure. Compensated for by adjusting the millibar scale to the datum required.

Temperature Error: The difference between actual temperature and its lapse rate and standard. If the air is colder than standard it will be more dense. The rate of decrease of pressure with height will therefore be greater. This will make the altimeter over-read and could be dangerous.

Blockages: Should the static ports become blocked (by insects, ice, etc.), the pressure inside the instrument case will remain constant and the altimeter will continue to read the height indicated when the blockage occurred. An alternative source of static pressure can be found by breaking the glass of a less important instrument – the vertical speed indicator (VSI). However, cabin static pressure is far from accurate and therefore all pressure instruments will be subject to considerable error.

Pilot's Serviceability Checks: When airfield pressure, QFE, is set on the millibar scale, the pointers should read zero, +/- fifty feet. If the pointers are within the permissible index error but not at zero, they should be turned to zero and a note made of the required correction to the millibar scale. This correction should then be applied to all subsequent altimeter settings.

TYPES OF ALTITUDE

Pilots are usually concerned with five types of altitude:

Indicated Altitude: This is the altitude displayed on the instrument above sea level when the appropriate datum is set. On the ground, with the altimeter set to airfield QNH, it should read airfield elevation assuming no instrument error. As soon as the helicopter becomes airborne it displays an indicated altitude because of non-standard temperature and pressure lapse rates with increasing altitude.

Pressure Altitude: This is an altitude measured above the standard pressure level, i.e. when 1013.2 millibars (29.92in) is set on the instrument. This altitude is used for computer solutions for true airspeed, density altitude, etc.

Density Altitude: This is pressure altitude corrected for non-standard temperature variations. A helicopter will have the same performance characteristics as it would have in standard atmosphere at this altitude. Density altitude is directly related to performance and many performance charts in the flight manual are based on density altitude.

True Altitude: This is the exact distance above mean sea level (AMSL). The altitude of all fixed objects is given in true altitude.

Absolute Altitude: This is the altitude of a helicopter above the surface of the terrain over which it is flying. This altitude may be abbreviated AGL – above ground level.

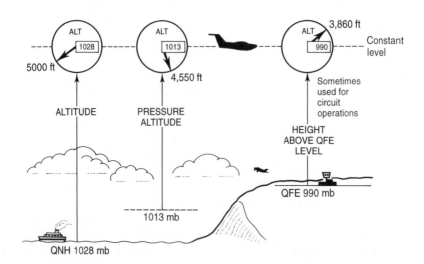

The altimeter reads height above whatever pressure level is set in the subscale.

Vertical Speed Indicator

The vertical speed indicator (VSI) is a sensitive differential pressure gauge. It records the rate of change of atmospheric pressure and displays it in terms of rate of climb or descent whenever the helicopter departs from level flight.

The instrument measures the difference of pressure between two chambers, one inside the other. Atmospheric pressure is fed directly into the inner chamber and through calibrated constrictions is allowed to leak into the outer chamber. When the atmospheric pressure changes, as when climbing or descending, the lag rate between the outer and inner chambers is a measure of the rate of climb or descent of the helicopter.

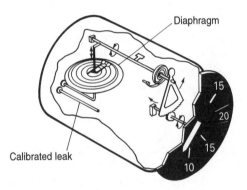

Vertical speed indicator

The instrument is required to give an accurate indication regardless of the effects of altitude and temperature. Compensation is achieved by incorporating in the metering unit both an orifice and a capillary, whose sizes are chosen so that the instrument readings remain correct over a wide range of altitude and temperature conditions.

The turbulent flow of air passing through an orifice slows down as altitude is increased and if this alone were used the instrument would under-read. The capillary, on the other hand, produces a laminar flow which increases its speed with altitude. Similar characteristics occur with variations in temperature; hence a subtle combination of the two devices can almost eliminate the effects of altitude and temperature.

Pressure Error: In a well-designed system this should be negligible.

Lag: After a sudden change to climb or descent, there will be a few seconds' delay in the reaction of the instrument.

Blockages: Any blockage of the helicopter's static system will render the instrument unserviceable and the pointer will remain at zero, irrespective of any vertical speed.

Pilot's Serviceability Checks: On the ground the instrument should read zero, +/- 200 feet per minute. In the air the instrument could be checked against a stopwatch if necessary.

The Airspeed Indicator

A knowledge of a helicopter's speed through the air is essential not only for safe handling but also for accurate navigation.

The airspeed indicator (ASI) is a sensitive differential pressure gauge operated by pressures picked up from the pitot-static system. When moved through the air, the pitot tube will pick up pitot pressure and feed it to one side of a sealed chamber divided by a thin flexible diaphragm. Static pressure is fed to the other side of this diaphragm which is subjected to two opposing pressures. Static pressures are balanced out so that any movement of the diaphragm is determined solely by the dynamic pressure. Movement of the diaphragm is transmitted through a mechanical linkage to a pointer on the face of the instrument where the dynamic pressure is indicated in terms of airspeed.

Most modern ASIs have a capsule instead of a diaphragm. The principle of operation is, however, exactly the same. Pitot pressure is fed to the inside of the capsule and static pressure to the outside. Pressure difference, therefore, causes the capsule to open out as airspeed increases. Since dynamic pressure varies not only with airspeed but also with air density and since air density varies with temperature and pressure (altitude), standard atmospheric values are used to calibrate the instrument.

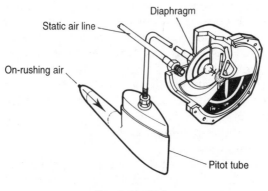

Airspeed indicator

Instrument and Pressure Errors: These are as discussed under altimeter errors.

Density Error: Since air density affects dynamic pressure, the ASI can only be calibrated to be accurate at one pressure level, i.e. sea level. Density decreases as height increases and the ASI will progressively under-read. Corrections can be calculated using the navigation computer.

Compressibility Error: At altitude air is more easily compressed than air at sea level. This causes an error which makes the ASI over-read at altitude. Increases in airspeed have the same effect. However, at the heights and airspeeds flown in general aviation compressibility error can be ignored.

Blockages and Leaks: If the pitot tube becomes blocked the ASI will not react to changes of airspeed. However, the capsule will act as a barometer, producing an apparent increase in airspeed if the helicopter climbs and an apparent decrease if the helicopter descends. If the static ports become blocked the ASI will over-read at lower altitudes and under-read at higher altitudes than that at which the blockage occurred. A leak in the pitot system causes the ASI to under-read. A leak in the static system will cause the ASI to over-read.

GYROSCOPES

A gyroscope consists of a symmetrical rotor spinning rapidly about its axis and free to rotate about one or more perpendicular axes. Freedom of movement about one axis is achieved by mounting the rotor in a gimbal. Complete freedom can be approached by using two gimbals.

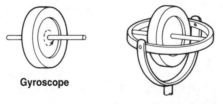

Gyroscope

Gyroscope with gimbals

The physical laws which govern the behaviour of a gyroscope are identical to those which account for the behaviour of the earth itself. The two principal properties of a gyroscope are RIGIDITY IN SPACE and PRECESSION. Both of these properties are exploited in helicopter instrument systems.

Rigidity in Space

The rotor inside a gyroscope maintains a constant attitude in space as long as no outside forces act upon it. This quality of stability is greater if the rotor has great mass and speed. Thus the gyros in helicopter instruments are of heavy construction and are designed to spin at high speeds.

Precession

This is the tilting or turning of the gyro axis in reaction to applied forces. When a deflective force is applied to the rim of a gyro rotor that *is not turning*, the rotor naturally moves in the direction of the force. However, when the gyro rotor *is rotating*, the same applied force causes the rotor to move in a direction as though the force had been applied at a point ninety degrees around the rim in the direction of rotation. This turning movement, or precession, places the rotor in a new plane of rotation.

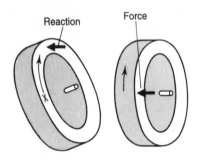

Precession

Unavoidable precessions are caused by manoeuvres and internal friction in the attitude and directional gyros. This causes slow drifting and minor erroneous indications in these instruments.

Gyroscopes are classified in terms of the quantity they measure. In aviation they are:

a) Displacement Gyroscopes, which measure angular displacement from a known datum and are used to define direction with respect to space.

b) Rate Gyroscopes, which measure the rate of angular displacements of a helicopter, e.g. the turn indicator.

c) Rate Integrating Gyroscopes, which measure the integral of an input with respect to time. This is the basis of most inertial navigation platforms.

THE ARTIFICIAL HORIZON

The artificial horizon with its miniature aircraft and horizon bar is the one instrument that portrays the picture of the actual attitude of the helicopter.

Because the horizon bar is connected to the gyro it remains parallel to the natural horizon. An adjustment knob is provided to move the miniature aircraft up and down inside the case. Normally it is adjusted so that the 'wings' overlap the horizon bar when the helicopter is in straight and level flight.

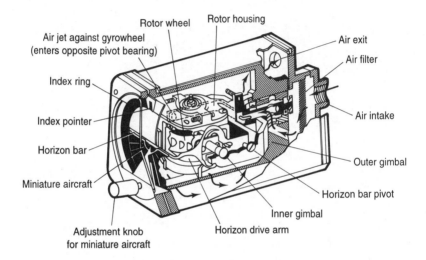

The artificial horizon gives an immediate indication of even the smallest changes in attitude and has no lead or lag. When the nose is raised above level attitude, the pictorial display shows the same attitude change in miniature. Besides showing attitude pitch changes, the instrument also shows movement about the longitudinal or roll axis. The instrument has an index mark at the top of the case which indicates the degree of bank by pointing to marks on either side of the instrument centreline. The small marks represent 10° of bank and the larger ones 30° of bank.

THE DIRECTIONAL GYRO

The directional gyro (DG), or heading indicator, is designed to operate without the magnetic errors inherent in the compass. It has no direction-seeking properties and must be set to headings shown on the magnetic compass. The directional gyro operates on the gyroscopic principle of rigidity in space with a vertical plane of rotation.

The compass rose card on the face of the instrument is linked to the gyro gimbal causing the card to turn as the helicopter turns. The pilot is able to turn a knob and adjust the card to the correct magnetic heading of the helicopter.

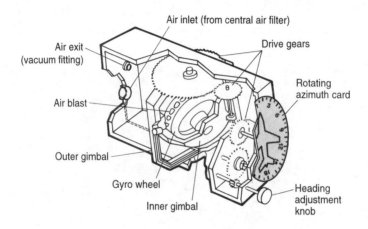

The directional gyro is subject to precession errors which cause the instrument to deviate from the correct magnetic heading. Whilst airborne the directional gyro should only be adjusted in straight and level flight or on the ground during run-up. Owing to precession errors it should be checked at least every fifteen minutes and reset as necessary.

THE TURN AND SLIP INDICATOR

The turn and slip indicator consists of two instruments contained in the same case. The turn indicator is a rate gyro mounted with its spin axis lying across the helicopter and indicates the rate at which the helicopter is turning about the yaw axis.

The gyro is mounted in a gimbal ring which is pivoted on each end and allows the gyro to rotate left and right. It is this freedom of movement that gives the gyro the ability to indicate a turn.

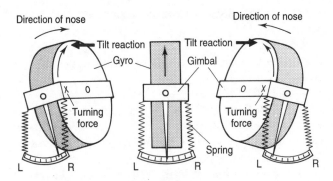

Turn indicator (diagrammatic)
From left to right: Turning right; Straight flight; Turning left

The slip indicator consists of a curved liquid-filled tube containing a ball. During a turn in which the helicopter's controls are properly co-ordinated, the ball will remain in the centre position. When the ball moves to the outside of the turn, a skid to the outside is indicated. When the ball moves to the inside of the turn, a slip to the inside of the turn is indicated. Either a skid or a slip means that the controls are not properly co-ordinated.

QUESTION AND ANSWERS

1. A pitot tube moving through the air senses:
   A) dynamic plus static pressure
   B) dynamic pressure only
   C) static pressure only
2. The airspeed indicator is connected to:
   A) the pitot pressure source only
   B) the vacuum system only
   C) both the pressure and static sources
3. The vertical speed indicator derives its reading from:
   A) the static source only
   B) the pitot source only
   C) the static and pitot sources
4. The following instrument is connected to the pitot pressure source:
   A) the altimeter
   B) the airspeed indicator
   C) the vertical speed indicator

5. If, in a climb, the static source becomes blocked, the altimeter would:
    A) be unaffected
    B) continue to indicate the altitude at which the blockage occurred
    C) over-read the altitude

6. An altimeter with the subscale set to aerodrome QFE will read:
    A) zero when the helicopter is on the ground at that aerodrome
    B) the height of the aerodrome above mean sea level
    C) the pressure altitude

7. At an aerodrome the altimeter settings are QNH 1007 and QFE 995 millibars. With the QNH set on the subscale and the altimeter reading 1,100 feet, the approximate vertical distance of the helicopter above the aerodrome would be:
    A) 750 feet
    B) 1,450 feet
    C) 360 feet

8. The 'ball' of a turn and slip indicator indicates:
    A) helicopter bank angle
    B) slip or skid
    C) the rate of turn of the helicopter

9. A rate of turn instrument would derive its information from:
    A) the precession of a gyro with its spin axis vertical
    B) the precession of a gyro with its spin axis horizontal
    C) the displacement of a weighted ball in a curved tube

10. The heading indication of a directional gyro:
    A) is always aligned with true north
    B) is always aligned with magnetic north
    C) requires readjustment by the pilot at regular intervals

ANSWERS

1. A	6. A
2. C	7. A
3. A	8. B
4. B	9. B
5. B	10. C

MAGNETISM AND COMPASSES

The magnetic compass was one of the first instruments to be fitted in an aircraft and is still the only direction-seeking instrument found in many light helicopters today.

The compass is a very reliable, self-contained unit and is independent of external power. To use it safely, however, the pilot must understand the principles of magnetism and the various errors common to compass operation.

BASIC PRINCIPLES

A magnet is a piece of metal that has the property of attracting another metal. The force of attraction is greatest at the poles (points near each end) of the magnet and least in the area halfway between. Lines of force flow from each of these poles in all directions, bending round and flowing towards the other pole to form a magnetic field.

The Earth acts as a huge magnet and the poles of this hypothetical magnet are known as the magnetic poles. Lines of magnetic force

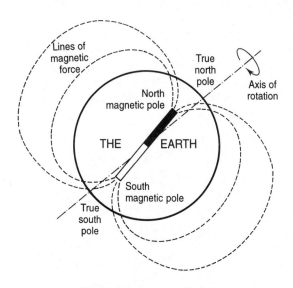

The Earth has a magnetic field

flow from each of these magnetic poles and, by so doing, form what is known as the Earth's magnetic field. Any freely suspended compass needle is deflected away from true direction by this hypothetical magnet and the direction indicated would be referred to as a magnetic direction.

The magnetic pole and the geographical (true) pole are some distance apart and, as a compass needle will align itself with the Earth's magnetic field, this will give a magnetic datum to measure from.

The angular difference between True North and Magnetic North is called MAGNETIC VARIATION. It is designated East or West according to whether the compass needle deflection is east or west of True North.

As variation is not constant over the Earth, places with the same variation are joined by lines called ISOGONALS. Variation changes continuously and against the isogonals printed on charts will be found the direction and amount of annual change. Each type of chart will show variation in different ways, so a close study of each chart is needed to determine how it is shown.

COMPASS CONSTRUCTION

The magnetic compass is located away from radios and electrical equipment to limit the effect of any magnetic disturbances in the helicopter. It contains a small internal light bulb for night illumination.

The compass card is graduated in 5° increments with the headings marked every 30°. The card is also equipped with a float to keep it horizontal in the compass fluid. A pivot underneath the card rests on a jewelled bearing which permits the card to rotate freely. Two long magnets mounted underneath give the compass its directional

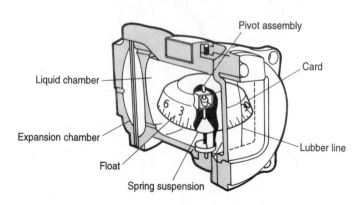

quality. These magnets always attempt to align themselves with the Earth's magnetic field.

The float assembly is sealed in a chamber filled with acid-free, white kerosene. This liquid serves several purposes. First, owing to buoyancy, part of the weight of the card is taken off the pivot which supports the card. Second, the fluid decreases the erratic swing of the compass, known as OSCILLATION. Third, the fluid lubricates the pivot point on a pedestal which serves as the mount for the float assembly and the compass card. The float assembly is balanced on the pivot, allowing free rotation of the card and a tilt of up to 18°.

At the rear of the compass bowl a diaphragm is installed to allow for any expansion or contraction of the liquid. This prevents the formation of bubbles or possible bursting of the case. Mounted behind the glass window is a reference line (lubber line) to designate the compass indication.

DEVIATION

Deviation is the deflection of the compass needle from a position of magnetic north as a result of local magnetic disturbance in the helicopter. Two small compensating magnets, adjustable by screws, are located in the top or bottom of the compass case to minimise deviation. Adjusting the compensating screws is known as 'swinging' the compass. The deviation noted should be recorded on a compass correction card.

FOR (MH)	0°	30°	60°	90°	120°	150°	180°	210°	240°	270°	300°	330°
STEER (CH)	359°	30°	60°	88°	120°	152°	183°	212°	240°	268°	300°	329°
RADIO ON ☒						RADIO OFF ☐						

Compass correction card

When flying compass headings, the pilot must refer to this card and make the appropriate adjustment for the desired heading. It is important to avoid placing metallic objects near the compass during flight, since this will induce large errors into the compass indications.

MAGNETIC DIP

Lines of force in the Earth's magnetic field are parallel to the Earth's surface at the Equator and curve increasingly downward closer to the magnetic poles.

The magnetic bars on the compass card tend to assume the same direction and position as the lines of magnetic force. Thus, the bars are parallel to the surface of the Earth at the magnetic equator while pointing increasingly downward closer to the magnetic poles. This characteristic, known as MAGNETIC DIP, is responsible for the northerly turning error and acceleration/deceleration error.

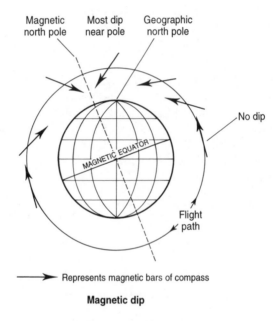

Magnetic dip

TURNING ERRORS

When the helicopter is banked, the compass card is also banked because of the centrifugal force acting upon it. While the compass card is in this banked position, the vertical components of the Earth's magnetic field cause the earth-seeking ends of the compass to dip to the low side of the turn and give an erroneous turn indication.

When the helicopter is making a turn on to north, the resultant indication is a lead into the direction of heading change. This will apply when turning through east or west on to a northerly heading. The correction is applied by rolling out of the turn when the compass reading is still some thirty degrees from north in the northern hemisphere.

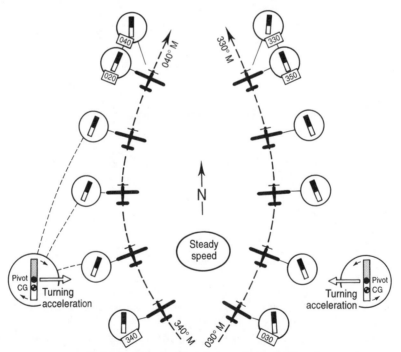

Undershoot the heading when turning through north

When turning on to a southerly heading the error is reversed in relation to the readings of the compass card, and the correction will be to roll out some 30° after the compass has indicated a southerly heading.

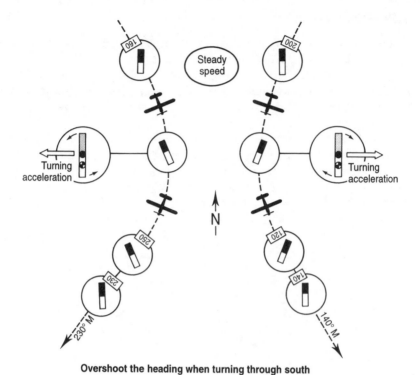

Overshoot the heading when turning through south

Turning errors are maximum when turning on to north or south and nil on to east or west.

ACCELERATION AND DECELERATION ERRORS

Acceleration and deceleration errors occur on easterly and westerly headings and are caused by a combination of inertia and the vertical component of the Earth's magnetic field.

Because of its pendulum-type mounting, the compass card tilts during airspeed changes. The momentary tilting of the card from the horizontal results in an error which is most apparent on easterly and westerly headings.

When accelerating on east or west an apparent turn towards north will be indicated when the helicopter is actually maintaining a constant heading.

Northern hemisphere

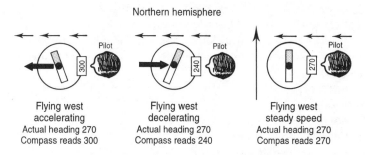

Flying west accelerating	Flying west decelerating	Flying west steady speed
Actual heading 270	Actual heading 270	Actual heading 270
Compass reads 300	Compass reads 240	Compas reads 270

Accelerating and decelerating on a westerly heading

When decelerating on easterly or westerly headings the apparent turn will be towards the south.

Northern hemisphere

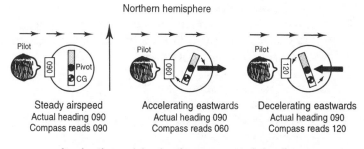

Steady airspeed	Accelerating eastwards	Decelerating eastwards
Actual heading 090	Actual heading 090	Actual heading 090
Compass reads 090	Compass reads 060	Compass reads 120

Accelerating and decelerating on an easterly heading

If the errors and characteristics are fully understood, the magnetic compass offers a reliable means of determining the heading of the helicopter. To read the compass accurately the helicopter must be flown level and at a steady airspeed.

QUESTIONS AND ANSWERS

1. For a constant rate of turn in the UK, turning errors in a magnetic compass are minimum as the helicopter turns through:
   A) north and south
   B) north-east, south-east, south-west and north-west
   C) east and west
2. In making an anti-clockwise turn on to a southerly heading using a direct-reading magnetic compass over the UK, a pilot needs to stop the turn:
   A) when the desired heading is indicated

B) after the desired heading is indicated

C) before the desired heading is indicated

3. When flying straight and level over the UK, the magnetic compass will indicate a turn to the left if speed is decreased when heading:

A) northerly

B) westerly

C) easterly

4. At the magnetic equator:

A) compass deviation is nil

B) variation is nil

C) dip is nil

5. Which of the following statements is correct:

A) annual changes on the charts apply to deviation

B) deviation is the angle between the true north pole and the magnetic north pole

C) the deviation of a compass can change on a long flight

6. Compass deviation cards mounted in the cockpit are required to indicate the difference between:

A) compass north and true north

B) compass readings and magnetic readings

C) true north and magnetic north

7. A large bunch of keys placed near the compass would affect:

A) the variation

B) the deviation

C) neither the variation nor the deviation

8. Above 70°N latitude, the compass is useless because:

A) variation is too large

B) the needle will not stay horizontal

C) the liquid expands

ANSWERS

1. C	2. B	3. B	4. C
5. C	6. B	7. C	8. B

4

BASIC HYDRAULICS

FUNDAMENTALS OF HYDRAULICS

INTRODUCTION

Hydraulics is the branch of science which deals with the properties of liquids and how they can be used to do work. In aircraft, hydraulic systems are used to operate controls, landing gear, wheel brakes, etc.

FLUID FLOW

When a fluid flows through a tube, it rubs against the wall of the tube. This holds some of the liquid back by resistance. Whenever there is a resistance there is a loss of energy. As the velocity of a moving liquid increases, the resistance also increases.

There are two kinds of fluid flow, LAMINAR and TURBULENT.

Laminar: When a liquid is forced through a constant-diameter tube at low velocity the flow is smooth and even, the fluid's particles tending to move in a parallel stream.

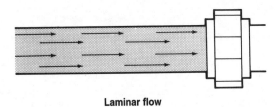

Laminar flow

The portion of liquid that touches the walls of the tube is slowed down because of friction. This means that the fluid near the centre of the tube moves at a higher velocity than does the outer portion of the liquid. However, as long as the velocity remains low, the flow will continue smooth because of the low resistance.

Turbulent: Resistance to a moving liquid is proportional to its velocity. When the velocity passes a critical point, the resistance increases until turbulent flow results.

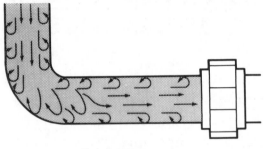

Turbulent flow

The velocity of a liquid in a tube is inversely proportional to the pressure in the tube. Should the liquid pass around a bend or through a restrictor, or should the tube's diameter suddenly decrease, the pressure will decrease and the velocity increase. This increased velocity can increase the resistance until turbulent flow results.

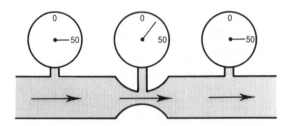

Fluid flow through orifice

PASCAL'S LAW

Pascal's Law, formulated by the Frenchman Blaise Pascal in the seventeenth century, expresses the basic principles of hydraulics. It states that a confined body of fluid exerts equal pressure at every point and in every direction in the fluid and it acts at right angles to the enclosing walls of the container with any increase in pressure.

HYDROSTATIC PARADOX

The pressure produced by a column of liquid is directly proportional to the height of the column and does not depend on the shape of the container.

For example, a tube that is 231 inches high with a one square inch cross-section will hold one US gallon of water. When the tube is standing upright, the one gallon of water exerts a pressure of 8.34 pounds per square inch (psi) at the bottom of the tube.

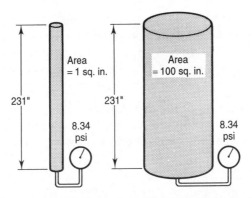

The pressure exerted by a column of liquid is determined by the height of the column and is independent of its volume.

The size or shape of the container holding the liquid makes no dif-ference. The volume of the container has also no effect on the pressure at the bottom – only the height of the column of liquid has this effect.

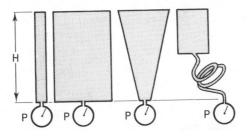

Neither the shape nor the volume of a container affects the pressure. Only the height of the column does this.

CHARACTERISTICS OF LIQUIDS

For all practical purposes liquids are regarded as being incom-pressible. This means that the volume of any given quantity will remain constant even though it is subjected to high pressure.

It has been proved that a force of 15 lb on a cubic inch of water will only decrease its volume by 1/20,000. It would take a force of some 32 tons to reduce it 10%.

RELATIONSHIP OF PRESSURE, FORCE AND AREA

In dealing with fluids, the terms FORCE and PRESSURE are used frequently, usually in relation to the areas over which they are applied.

Force may be defined as a push or a pull. It is the push or pull exerted against the total area of a particular surface acted upon. In hydraulics, this unit area is expressed in pounds per square inch. This pressure is the amount of force acting upon one square inch of area.

Computing Pressure, Force and Area

A formula is used to compute pressure, force and area in fluid power systems and can easily be remembered by expressing it as:

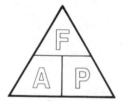

In this formula, P refers to pressure, F indicates force and A represents area. Thus $F = A \times^* P$, $A = F \div P$, and $P = F \div A$.

Consider the effect in the system shown below in which the column of fluid is curved back up to its original level and fitted with a piston at each end.

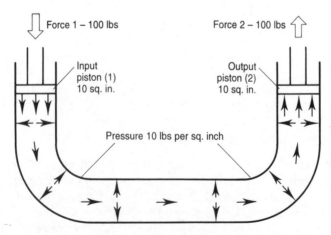

Force 1 – 100 lbs   Force 2 – 100 lbs

Input piston (1) 10 sq. in.   Output piston (2) 10 sq. in.

Pressure 10 lbs per sq. inch

Force transmitted through fluid

If there is a resistance on the output piston (2) and the input piston (1) is pushed down, a pressure is created through the fluid acting equally at right angles to the surfaces in all parts of the container.

Suppose the area of the input piston (1) is ten square inches and the down force is 100 lb, then the pressure in the fluid is 10 psi (100 ÷ 0). It must be emphasised that this pressure cannot be created without resistance to flow which, in this case, is provided by the 100 lb force acting against the top of the output piston (2). This pressure acts on piston (2), so that for each square inch of its area it is pushed upwards with a force of 10 lb. Therefore, the upward force on the output piston is the same as the input piston. All that has been accomplished in this system was to transmit the 100 lb force around a bend.

Since Pascal's Law is independent of the shape of the container, it is not necessary that the tube connecting the two pistons should be the full cross-sectional area of the pistons. A connection of any size, shape or length will do so long as an unobstructed passage is provided.

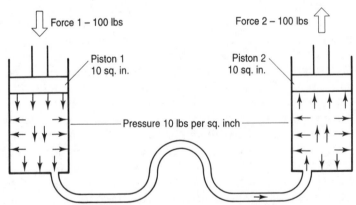

Transmitting force through small pipe

Therefore, the system shown above will act exactly the same as the previous one.

MULTIPLICATION OF FORCES

If two pistons are used in a fluid power system, the force acting on each is directly proportional to its area, and the magnitude of each force is the product of the pressure and its area.

Another consideration is the distance the pistons move and the volume of the fluid displaced.

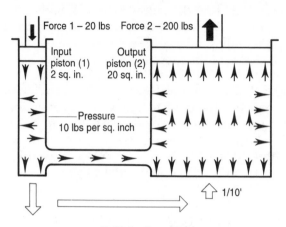

Multiplication of forces

Consider the above situation. An input piston with an area of two square inches travels through a distance to create a movement of the much larger, twenty-square-inch, output piston. If the input piston is pushed down one inch, only two cubic inches of fluid are displaced. In order to accommodate these two cubic inches of fluid, the output piston will have to move only 1/10th of an inch because its area is ten times that of the input piston. However, the input force of only 20 lb will produce a lifting force (the resistance) of 200 lb. This is the principle on which the hydraulic jack is based.

An increase in force can only be obtained by a proportional decrease in distance travelled. A distance increase can be obtained, but only at the expense of a force decrease in the same ratio. This leads us to the basic statement: 'Neglecting friction, in any fluid power system the input force multiplied by the distance through which it moves is always exactly equal to the output force multiplied by the distance through which it travels.'

The relationship of volume, area and length is easily expressed:

Relationship of volume, area, and length

Hydraulic Fluids

Manufacturers of hydraulic devices usually specify the type of fluid best suited for use in their equipment. Their recommendations are based on the working conditions, temperatures expected, pressures the fluid must withstand and the possibility of corrosion.

VISCOSITY

One of the most important properties of a liquid to be used in an hydraulic system is its viscosity. Viscosity is the internal resistance of a fluid which tends to prevent it flowing. A liquid such as gasoline has a low viscosity, while tar, which flows slowly, has a high viscosity. The viscosity of a liquid is affected by changes in temperature – it flows more easily when hot than when cold. A good hydraulic fluid will have a low viscosity at all temperatures.

CHEMICAL STABILITY

Chemical stability is another property important to the selection of hydraulic fluids. It is defined as the liquid's ability to resist oxidation and deterioration for long periods.

FLASHPOINT

This is the temperature at which a liquid gives off vapour in sufficient quantity to ignite momentarily or flash when a flame is applied. A high flashpoint is desirable for hydraulic fluid because it provides a good resistance to combustion.

FIREPOINT

Firepoint is the temperature at which a substance gives off vapour in sufficient quantity to ignite and continue to burn when exposed to a spark or flame. Like flashpoint, a high firepoint is required of hydraulic fluids.

TYPES OF HYDRAULIC FLUIDS

Many different liquids have been tested for use in hydraulic systems. The liquids presently in use include mineral oil, vegetable oil and phosphate esters. Hydraulic fluids are usually classified according to their type of base.

CONTAMINATION

Many different types of contamination are harmful to hydraulic fluids but they generally fall into two classes:

Abrasives: These include sand core particles, machine chips, rust, etc.

Non-abrasives: Soft particles from worn or shredded seals and other organic components. The origin of contamination can usually be traced to four major areas:

a) particles originally contained in the system from fabrication and storage of system components

b) particles introduced from outside sources, such as reservoir or breather vents

c) particles created within the system during operation by frictional wear or contact in components, pumps, cylinders, etc.

d) particles introduced by foreign liquids. One of the most common is water which normally settles to the bottom of the reservoir

System filters usually provide adequate control of the contamination problem.

Hydraulic System Components

RESERVOIRS

The reservoir is a tank in which an adequate supply of fluid for the system is stored. Fluid flows from the reservoir to the pump(s), where it is forced through the system, eventually returning to the reservoir. The reservoir not only supplies the operating needs of the system but also replenishes fluid lost through leakage. It also serves as an overflow basin for excess fluid forced out of the system by thermal expansion, by the accumulator and by piston and rod displacement.

Non-pressurised Reservoirs

Most non-pressurised reservoirs are used in aircraft that fly only in the lower altitudes. The reservoirs must be large enough to hold all the fluid for any condition of the hydraulic system.

An air port on the top serves as an overboard vent which allows the reservoir to 'breathe'. This prevents a vacuum forming as the fluid level lowers inside the reservoir. It also allows any air which has entered the system to escape. The reservoir will have a filter to keep the fluid free of foreign matter. Filters are usually located in the filler neck and are of the screen mesh type.

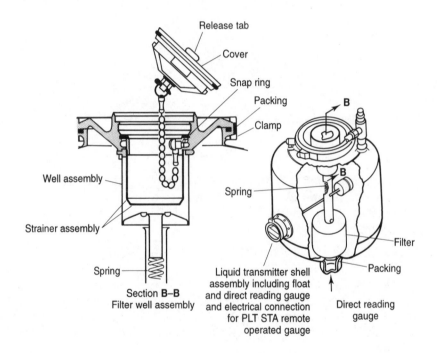

A sight glass gives a visual indication of the amount of fluid in the reservoir.

Pressurised Reservoirs

The reservoirs on aircraft designed to fly at high altitudes are usually pressurised. Pressurisation assures a positive flow of fluid to the pumps at high altitudes, where low atmospheric pressures are encountered.

One method of pressurisation uses an aspirator in the return line from the main system to the reservoir. As the fluid flows through the aspirator it pulls in air from the cabin by jet action and mixes it with the returning fluid. A pressure regulator, or relief valve, maintains reservoir pressure within a predetermined range.

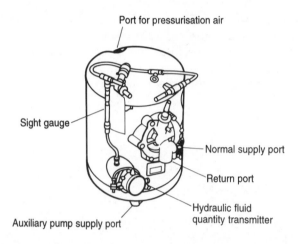

Hydraulic reservoir pressurised with air

Another method uses engine bleed air to maintain a pressure of up to 40-45 psi in the main reservoirs. An air pressure regulator is used to limit the engine bleed air to a desired range within the reservoir.

FILTRATION

Many malfunctions in hydraulic systems can be attributed to some type of fluid contamination. Because of the extremely small clearances between component parts in many hydraulic pumps and valves, the importance of keeping the fluid clean cannot be over-emphasised.

Pressure and return-line filters normally consist of a filter case, head, filter element and a bypass or relief valve. The case contains the element and screws into the head which incorporates the 'in' and 'out' ports as well as the relief/bypass valve. The normal fluid flow through this type of filter is through the 'in' port, around the outside of the element, through the element to the inner chamber and then out through the 'out' port.

The filter element is made of a specially treated cellulose paper and is commonly known as a MICRONIC FILTER. Other elements may comprise sintered metal (bronze) woven wire or a one-piece

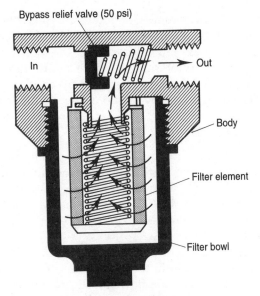

Full flow hydraulic filter

corrugated wire mesh of stainless steel. The paper cellulose element and some of the stainless steel woven mesh elements are wrapped around a spring-type frame to prevent collapse as the fluid flows through.

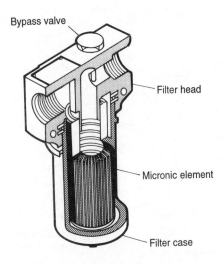

Micronic-type filter, using a paper element

Should these filters become clogged, the bypass or relief valve in the filter head will open, allowing a flow of unfiltered fluid. Some filter units use a bypass indicator to alert the operator of a bypass (clogged element) or differential pressure situation. The pin or button on top of the head will protrude from the filter housing. The element should then be removed and either cleaned or exchanged.

COOLER RADIATORS

Hydraulic systems operate most efficiently when the fluid temperature is held within a specific range. Temperatures higher than the desired level reduce the lubricating characteristics of the fluid and cause the fluid to break down, forming a sludge. In most systems, cold fluid may cause a sluggish action of the fluid when the system is first operated.

The component used to cool the hydraulic fluid in most helicopters is the hydraulic fluid radiator. This is similar in design to a car radiator in which the fluid flows through small tubes in the core and air is forced through the honeycomb material to cool the liquid.

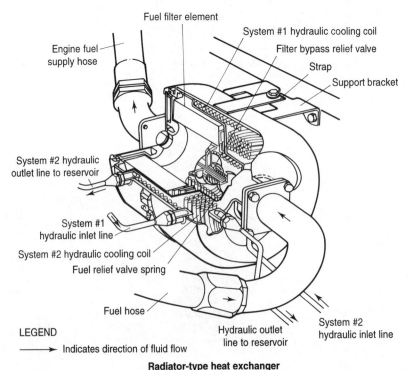

Radiator-type heat exchanger

HYDRAULIC PUMPS

All aircraft systems have one or more power-driven pumps. Pumps are simply fluid movers: they generate the flow of fluid. Pressure will only be generated when there is a restriction to the flow.

Power-driven pumps are the primary source of energy and on helicopters are usually driven from the main transmission.

Power-driven pumps are classified according to the type of pumping action utilised and may be either gear-type or piston-type. They may be further classified according to whether they are designed for CONSTANT DISPLACEMENT or VARIABLE DISPLACEMENT. A constant-displacement pump is one that displaces or delivers a constant fluid output for any rotational speed. A variable-displacement pump has a fluid output that varies to meet the demands of the system.

PRESSURE REGULATORS

Pressure regulators, sometimes called 'unloading' valves, are used in hydraulic systems to unload the pump and to regulate system operating pressure.

A pressure regulator is said to be in the 'kicked-in' position when it is directing fluid under pressure into the system. In the 'kicked-out' position, the fluid in the system downstream of the regulator is trapped at the desired pressure and the fluid from the pump is bypassed into the return line and back to the reservoir.

ACCUMULATORS

The accumulator serves as a cushion or shock absorber by maintaining an even pressure in the system. It also stores enough fluid under pressure for emergency operation of certain actuating units. The accumulator also supplements the pump's output under peak loads by storing energy in the form of fluid under pressure. Accumulators are designed with a compressed air chamber separated from the fluid by a flexible diaphragm, a flexible bladder or a moveable piston.

HYDRAULIC ACTUATORS

An actuator is a device which converts fluid power into mechanical force and motion.

An actuating cylinder is a device which converts fluid power to linear or straight-line force and motion. Since linear motion is a back and forth motion along a straight line, this type of actuator is sometimes referred to as RECIPROCATING. Actuating cylinders are normally installed in such a way that the cylinder is anchored to a stationary structure and the piston is attached to the mechanism to be operated.

A servo actuator is designed to provide hydraulic power to move various aircraft controls. They usually include an actuating cylinder, a flow control valve, check valves and relief valves.

A simple Hydraulic System

Normally, a piston is fitted in a small cylinder to exert pressure on fluid in a connecting pipe to a larger cylinder, also fitted with a piston. The smaller cylinder is called the MASTER CYLINDER and the larger one the ACTUATING CYLINDER.

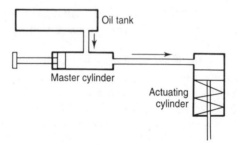

To prevent the fluid rushing back into the master cylinder, a non-return valve (NRV) is fitted between the master and actuating cylinders.

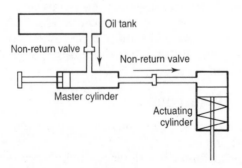

The fluid in the system is now held under pressure.

In order that the pressure can be released to allow the piston to move the other way, a return line must be introduced together with a selector valve. To operate the system at working pressure, a power pump must be included together with a pressure relief valve (PRV).

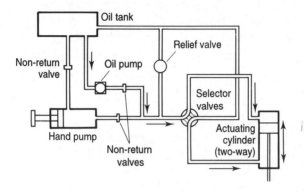

Bell 206 JetRanger Hydraulic System

The hydraulic system consists of a pump, reservoir and pressure regulator mounted in one assembly on the front of the transmission and three servo actuators with irreversible valves.

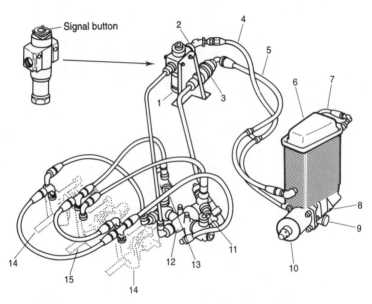

1. Filter
2. Quick-disconnect socket (pressure)
3. Quick-disconnect socket (return)
4. Hose (pressure)
5. Hose (return)
6. Pump and reservoir
7. Vent line
8. Vent
9. Pressure regulator valve
10. Tachometer generator
11. Cap
12. Cap
13. Solenoid valve
14. Servo actuator (cyclic)
15. Servo actuator (collective)

The pump is driven by the transmission oil pump shaft, and so provides for the availability of fully boosted flight controls during autorotation. The reservoir assembly contains a transparent plastic sight glass on the side to allow for a quick visual check of the fluid

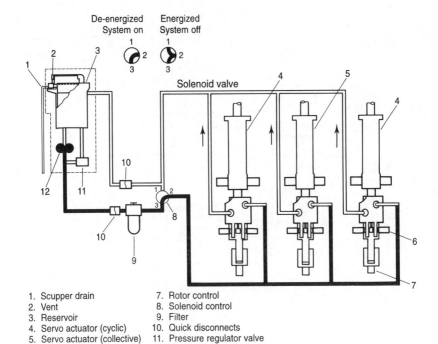

De-energized System on
Energized System off

Solenoid valve

1. Scupper drain
2. Vent
3. Reservoir
4. Servo actuator (cyclic)
5. Servo actuator (collective)
6. Pilot input
7. Rotor control
8. Solenoid control
9. Filter
10. Quick disconnects
11. Pressure regulator valve
12. Pump

level and has a capacity of one US pint. A bypass valve and filter element near the right-hand side of the system incorporates a red button which 'pops' up to warn of a dirty filter condition.

Just forward of the pump assembly is a solenoid valve which permits or prevents the flow of fluid in the system, depending on the selected position. It is electrically operated by a switch on the pedestal. The system operates at 600 psi ± 25 psi (4,137 ± 172 kilopascals).

The irreversible valves on the servo actuators isolate the servo system from the flight controls in the case of an hydraulic malfunction. If a malfunction occurs, the flight control motions remain the same but the force required to move them increases. The rate at which they can be changed is slightly decreased.

The pilot can isolate the system by turning it off and can continue with the flight because the feedback through the flying controls is not excessive. For this reason a back-up system is not required.

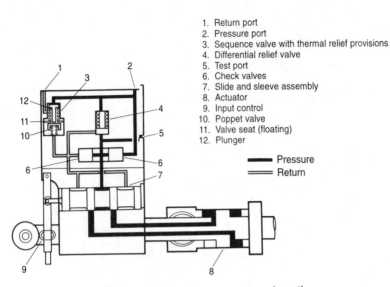

1. Return port
2. Pressure port
3. Sequence valve with thermal relief provisions
4. Differential relief valve
5. Test port
6. Check valves
7. Slide and sleeve assembly
8. Actuator
9. Input control
10. Poppet valve
11. Valve seat (floating)
12. Plunger

━━━ Pressure
══ Return

Cyclic and collective servo actuator schematic

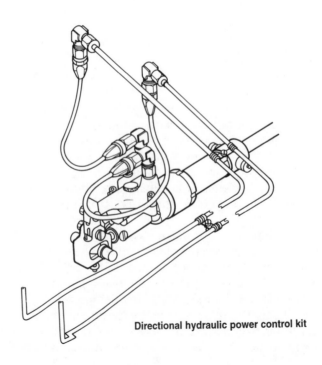

Directional hydraulic power control kit

For normal flight conditions, hydraulic boost is not merited for the tail-rotor controls. When boost is desirable on all flight controls, a directional hydraulic power control kit is available which adds the boost to the tail-rotor control system and forms an integral part of the main system. The kit consists of a cylinder and support assembly, check valve and hoses necessary for installation.
This kit adds approximately 7 lb (3 kg) to the basic weight of the helicopter.

QUESTIONS AND ANSWERS

1. With a system pressure of 3,000 psi, the force provided by a four-square-inch area jack compared with a two-square-inch area jack is:
   A) the same
   B) 6,000 lb greater
   C) 6,000 lb less
2. With a system pressure of 3,000 psi and a piston stroke of 5 in. the work done by a four-square-inch jack compared with a two-square-inch jack is:
   A) the same
   B) half as much
   C) twice as much
3. Hydraulic reservoirs are pressurised to:
   A) minimise the possibility of pump cavitation
   B) provide a reserve of stored energy
   C) maintain a constant fluid level
4. In a helicopter hydraulic system, it is permissible to use:
   A) any hydraulic fluid available
   B) only the specified fluid
   C) any fluid of the same specific gravity
5. In an hydraulic system of the constant-delivery type, essential components are an:
   A) accumulator and automatic cut-out valve
   B) accumulator and shuttle valve
   C) accumulator and relay valve
6. An automatic cut-out valve will:
   A) prevent an hydraulic lock forming
   B) limit pump wear
   C) raise fluid boiling point

7. One reason for fitting an accumulator in an hydraulic system is to:
   A) absorb pressure surges
   B) minimise the possibility of pump cavitation
   C) relieve excess pressure

8. A thermal relief valve is fitted to:
   A) prevent excess temperature
   B) relieve excess pressure
   C) prevent a leak back of pressure

9. Handpump fluid supply is drawn from:
   A) a stack pipe higher than normal fluid supply
   B) the bottom of the reservoir
   C) a stack pipe tapped into the top of the reservoir

10. A handpump is usually fitted to be used for:
    A) ground servicing and an emergency power source
    B) maintaining the fluid level of the reservoir
    C) ground charging of the air pressure in the accumulator and reservoir

11. Given the same pressure, a four-square-inch-area jack provides:
    A) twice as much force as a two-square-inch jack
    B) the same force as a two-square-inch jack
    C) half as much force as a two-square-inch jack

12. Given the same pressure and length of travel, a four-square-inch jack does:
    A) more work than a two-square-inch jack
    B) less work than a two-square-inch jack
    C) same work as a two-square-inch jack

13. The colour of fluid DTD 585 is:
    A) green
    B) blue
    C) red

14. If you have an emergency air bottle in an hydraulic system, it is used for:
    A) emergency operation of a system
    B) raising the level of fluid in the reservoir
    C) increasing the accumulator pressure

15. In a constant-flow delivery system, output is controlled by:
    A) an automatic cut-out valve
    B) a selector valve
    C) an accumulator

16. The effect of the off-load/on-load cycle of too high an air charge pressure in an accumulator would be that the:
    A) interval between would be reduced
    B) interval between would be increased
    C) interval between would remain the same

17. Thermal relief valves are set to:
    A) the same pressure as the ACOV cut-in
    B) the same pressure as the ACOV cut-out
    C) a higher pressure than the ACOV cut-out

18. Handpump emergency fluid supply is usually drawn from:
    A) the top of the reservoir
    B) the bottom of the reservoir
    C) a stack pipe in the reservoir

19. Handpumps in hydraulic systems are generally:
    A) double-acting
    B) rotary
    C) single-acting

20. A shuttle valve is used for:
    A) changeover from main to auxiliary system in the case of failure
    B) maintaining fluid pressure when the emergency system fails
    C) preventing fluid loss from a leaking jack

21. If a shuttle valve fails during normal operation:
    A) main braking is not available
    B) emergency braking is not available
    C) both systems will operate

22. A stuck shuttle valve will:
    A) prevent emergency fluid becoming available in a system
    B) prevent normal fluid becoming available in a system
    C) close off supply to a jack if pressure is low

23. When pressurising the accumulator you:
    A) operate the system to charge the accumulator with fluid
    B) empty the accumulator of fluid
    C) remove all air pressure

24. The effect of low air pressure in an accumulator is:
    A) rapid jack movements
    B) rapid fluctuations in pressure
    C) system pressure will be slow to build up

25. On a simple hydraulic system a selector valve is used to:
    A) normally raise or lower the undercarriage
    B) provide a direct air supply back to the reservoir to pressurise the fluid
    C) act as a pressure relief valve

26. If there is a fluid leakage from the jack:
    A) the jack lubrication system is working normally
    B) an oil seal has failed
    C) there are air bubbles in the fluid
27. Restrictor valves in a hydraulic system are used to:
    A) limit the maximum pressure
    B) control the rate of system operation
    C) restrict the rate of pressure build-up
28. Hydraulic accumulator air pressure can be checked:
    A) with the system pressurised only
    B) with the system depressurised only
    C) at any time
29. Low air pressure in a brake accumulator will cause the number of full brake applications available to:
    A) increase
    B) decrease
    C) remain the same
30. The effect of an external leak in a system could be to:
    A) cause loss of fluid content
    B) lose system pressure and cause overheating
    C) cause loss of fluid content and pressure, overheating and possible fire hazard
31. Bleeding of the hydraulic system is:
    A) taking all the contents from the system
    B) removing particles from the system
    C) removing air from the system
32. To check the air pressure of an hydraulic system accumulator, the:
    A) accumulator residual air pressure must be exhausted
    B) accumulator must be charged with fluid by the system
    C) accumulator fluid content must be exhausted
33. The purpose of an hydraulic reservoir is to:
    A) allow the engineer to check that the fluid is in the system
    B) allow for jack movements, thermal expansion and small leaks
    C) pressurise the system
34. Sluggish operation of hydraulic services is caused by:
    A) air in the system
    B) too high air pressure in the system accumulator
    C) air trapped in the reservoir under pressure

35. In an hydraulic tank with an aperture in the side, the head of fluid is:
    A) the amount of fluid above the aperture subtracted from the total depth
    B) the tank capacity divided by the fluid depth
    C) the fluid from the aperture to the leak of fluid

Answers

1. B	11. A	21. B	31. C
2. C	12. A	22. A	32. C
3. A	13. C	23. A	33. B
4. B	14. A	24. C	34. A
5. A	15. A	25. A	35. C
6. B	16. A	26. B	
7. A	17. C	27. B	
8. B	18. B	28. B	
9. B	19. A	29. B	
10. A	20. A	30. C	

5

AN INTRODUCTION TO GAS TURBINE ENGINES

To understand the working of a gas turbine engine it is essential to understand the principles of reaction propulsion motors such as ROCKETS, RAM JETS and PULSE JETS, together with some basic gas laws and the purpose of components such as COMPRESSORS and TURBINES.

Isaac Newton laid down three laws of motion, of which the third one states: 'For every action there is an equal and opposite reaction.' The jet engine is based on this law.

A Rocket motor uses solid or liquid fuel as a propellant which, when burnt, produces rapidly expanding gases which can only discharge rearward. This force rearward is equalled by a force pushing forward. Therefore, the more gas accelerated rearward the greater will be the force forward. We can then say that the mass of gas accelerated is equal to the thrust forward.

Charge a tube with air and fuel, close one end and ignite it. Expansion will take place and the gas will be discharged – thrust results. Open the closed end, recharge and the cycle could begin again.

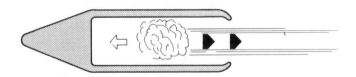

To make a jet engine start with a tube. The shape of the tube is based upon the venturi principle. A venturi has a CONVERGENT DUCT guiding incoming air and a DIVERGENT DUCT guiding outgoing air. Air passing through a convergent duct will speed up and the pressure will decrease proportionally. Air passing through a divergent duct will slow down and the pressure will increase proportionally. With pressure increase temperature will also increase, and vice versa.

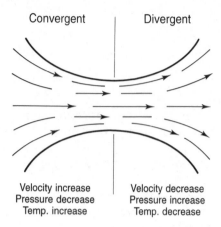

Convergent | Divergent

Velocity increase
Pressure decrease
Temp. increase

Velocity decrease
Pressure increase
Temp. decrease

If we arrange the shape of the tube so that the air first passes through a divergent duct and then through a convergent duct, we have the basic shape of jet engines.

Note that at point (a) there will be a pressure increase and at (c) a pressure decrease. If we heat the area (b) expansion will take place, the pressure moving towards the low pressure area (c) to be discharged at a higher velocity at the outlet than at the inlet.

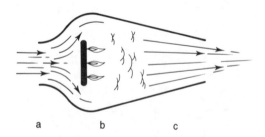

a   b   c

The difference in velocities must be how much air has been accelerated and, as seen previously MASS × ACCELERATION = THRUST. A simple duct shaped thus, burning fuel to cause expansion, is known as an AERO THERMAL DYNAMIC DUCT (ATHODYD).

To get the air inside the tube by moving it forward would require high speed if the pressure at (b) is not overcome by the pressure at (a). To overcome this a Pulse Jet was used (German V1 flying bomb) which had front doors that opened to let in fresh air and closed when expansion due to burning took place. The familiar 'pop-pop' noise was due to the regular cycle of the engine's combustion phase.

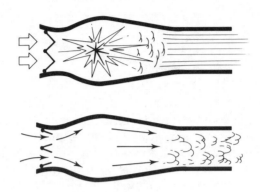

Ram Jets are more sophisticated athodyds that could be designed to operate between the 600-2,000 mph range.

It can be seen, therefore, that air must enter the tube in another way if it is to operate at low forward speed. The answer is to draw in the air and bring it to a working pressure using a compressor.

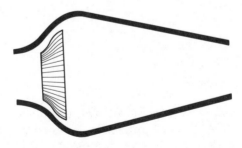

The compressor must be rotated by mechanical means and many methods have been used in the past. The most successful method is to drive the compressor by a turbine deriving its energy from the exhaust gas stream.

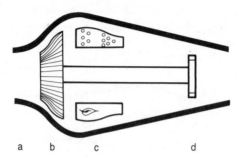

a   b   c   d

Once the engine has started it is self-supporting. The flame must be controlled and contained, and this takes place inside the combustion chamber. The flame is very hot inside the tube (approximately 2,000°C), and must be kept away from the metal.

Total airflow can be divided into three: PRIMARY for combustion, SECONDARY for shaping the flame and TERTIARY for cooling. About one third of the airflow is used for combustion and the rest for cooling. The hot gases rush towards the exit and must be cooled to around 850°C before they hit the turbines.

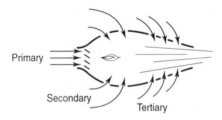

The turbine is made of Nimonic alloy and is able to withstand very high temperatures. If the temperature becomes excessive the turbine blades may distort or stretch (creep). If this occurs, serious mechanical failure could result and this is why a temperature limitation is stipulated.

A turbine wheel has blades set at an angle to the axis, so that when the gases hit or impinge on the blade the force tends to move the turbine wheel around its axis. Each time the gas strikes the blades a force is set up, the shape of the blade being such so as to accept the force. This is known as IMPULSE BLADING.

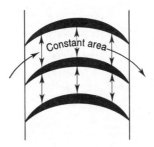

Impulse turbine blading

If the turbine blades are shaped so that the exhaust from the blades is directed away from the rotation of the wheel and the gap between the blades is made convergent, then the accelerating outlet gases will give a resultant force assisting the turning force. This is known as REACTION BLADING.

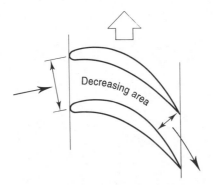

Reaction turbine blading

To increase the efficiency of the turbine there is normally a marriage between the two types of blading.

As it is the force of the moving gas that turns the turbine, to increase output and efficiency the gas must be directed at the best angle and the velocity increased. This is achieved by NOZZLE GUIDE VANES (NGVs) set just before the turbine blades. For each set of turbine blades there is a set of nozzle guide vanes.

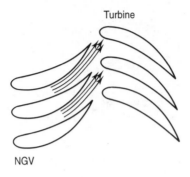

There are two basic types of compressor used on gas turbine engines, AXIAL and CENTRIFUGAL. The most common type is the centrifugal compressor, in which air drawn in is pushed outward at high speed by centrifugal force and velocity increases. To obtain the pressure the air is led through a unit called a DIFFUSER which, being a divergent duct, changes velocity to pressure.

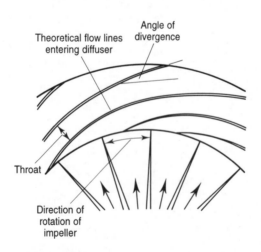

Airflow at entry to diffuser showing divergent passages

Therefore, a compressor must be inclusive of a method of changing velocity to pressure. This applies equally to axial compressors.

An axial compressor accelerates the air along and in line with the axis of its shaft. Downstream of the compressor blades are DIVERGENT STATOR BLADES which change velocity to pressure.

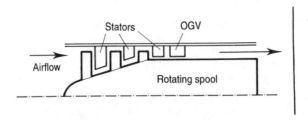

To summarise, a gas turbine engine will supply energy in the form of accelerated gases at low forward speed. The gases can then be used as pure jet reaction propulsion or to drive a turbine. If the turbine is attached to a driveshaft and is not coupled to a compressor, it is known as a FREE TURBINE.

GAS TURBINES – GENERAL

INTRODUCTION

The gas turbine was developed for aircraft use to overcome the problems of high-speed and high-altitude flying. It is also a very simple engine with few moving parts when compared with a piston engine, which gives it a high reliability factor with little maintenance. Another advantage is a higher power/weight ratio, some three times better than that of the piston engine.

The working cycle of a gas turbine engine is similar to that of a piston engine in that there is induction, compression, combustion and exhaust. With the piston engine combustion (power) is intermittent whereas in the gas turbine each process is continuous.

The gas turbine has a separate compressor, combustion system, turbine assembly and exhaust system, with each part concerned only with its own function. Combustion takes place at constant pressure. The absence of reciprocating parts provides a much-smoother-running engine of lighter construction, enabling more energy to be released for useful propulsive work.

PRINCIPLES OF JET PROPULSION

The propeller produces thrust by accelerating a comparatively large cold mass to a moderate velocity, whereas the jet engine is a reaction engine that takes in at the front a continuous small mass of air, heats it up and causes it to accelerate at high velocity. This movement of air is governed by Newton's Laws of Motion and in particular the third law, which states, 'A reaction will be produced, equal to the force applied but acting in the opposite direction.'

In a jet engine the force applied is the acceleration of the air mass. The reaction is the thrust produced by the engine in a forward direction. The velocity change in the airflow between the air inlet and the exhaust outlet can be used to calculate the size of the force. The airflow's mass multiplied by its velocity change gives the value of thrust: MASS × ACCELERATION = THRUST.

THE JET ENGINE

The modern jet engine is basically cylindrical in shape because it is essentially a duct. Into this duct are fitted the necessary parts.

The parts from front to rear are the compressor, the combustion system, the turbine assembly and the exhaust system. A shaft connects the turbine to the compressor and fuel burners are positioned in the combustion system. Ignition is provided once the airflow is produced by rotating the compressor. The pressure of the mass ensures that the expanding gas travels rearward. A starter is used to initiate rotation of the compressor.

Once ignition is achieved, the flame will be continuous provided fuel is supplied; the ignition device can be turned off. Because the hot gases crossing the turbine produce torque to drive the compressor, the starter can also be turned off.

Types of Engine

A number of different types of engine have been produced, each to do a specific job more efficiently. They are all basically similar, the differences being in the type of compressors used, the type of combustion system and the method of propulsion.

Engines are classified by these differences as follows:

a)   centrifugal (one or two stages) jets or gas turbines
b)   axial flow (one-, two- or three-spool) jets or gas turbines
c)   bypass engines (twin-spool)
d)   ducted fan engines (twin- or triple-spool)
e)   turboprop engines: direct coupled, free turbine, compound
f)   helicopter engines (very similar to turboprops)

Centrifugal-type compressors were used on the early engines and then were superseded by the axial-flow type. Modern engines however, may use a combination of both types.

Generally speaking, jet engines are used for high-speed, high-altitude aircraft; bypass engines for high subsonic speed, ducted fans for medium speed and turboprop for the lower-speed aircraft. The turbine may also provide drive for other items such as fuel pumps, hydraulic pumps, generators, and any other engine accessories.

Airflow

Air drawn in at the intake enters the compressor, where its pressure and temperature is increased without change to its final velocity. During the combustion process heat energy is added by burning fuel, but no pressure increase takes place; the energy is converted into velocity. This increase in heat energy and velocity energy is used to produce torque at the turbine. Any pressure energy in the gas can also be used to assist in producing torque from the turbine by suitable blade design.

After leaving the turbine assembly, the remaining energy of the mass flow of hot gases can be used to produce thrust. Its velocity is kept at a high value so that exit velocity, being higher than intake velocity, gives an acceleration change and therefore a thrust value equal to mass (pounds per second) × acceleration (difference between intake/outlet velocities in feet per second). The remaining gas stream energy after the compressor-driving turbines may be used to drive other turbines, propellers, rotors or any other means of propulsion. In these cases the engines are not 'jet' engines but 'gas turbines', the engine becoming a gas generator providing energy to drive 'power take-off' turbines.

COMPRESSORS

INTRODUCTION

A propulsion unit designed to produce thrust by reaction need not require a compressor, e.g. a ram jet, air mass flow being provided in this case by ram effect, that is to say by the unit passing through the air at very high speed. Because of the low pressure achieved in this way, these units are inefficient and have a high fuel consumption. No thrust is produced when the unit is static, so to produce a large mass of flow at pressure some form of air pump is necessary.

The compressor provides this mass flow and at the same time increases its pressure. Although the pressure has little bearing on the mass, it does improve the rate at which energy can be released from the burning fuel. To a large extent high compression pressures have a similar effect to high compression ratios in piston engines.

Basically two types of compressor are used in gas turbines, CENTRIFUGAL VANE types and AXIAL FLOW types.

CENTRIFUGAL COMPRESSORS

This type is similar to the supercharger used in piston engines, comprising a disc on which is formed a number of radially spaced vanes. Around this disc, or IMPELLER, is a ring of stationary vanes formed with divergent cross-sections between them.

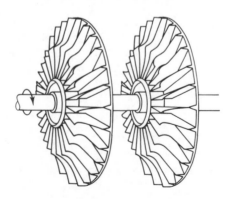

Multi-stage compressor impeller assembly

When driven at high speed, the air at the disc centre is forced radially outward along the vanes of the disc. This rotational energy of the disc imparts velocity energy to the air because of the divergent passage. Some of this energy is converted into pressure and temperature.

Leaving the impeller tip at high speed, the air enters the diffuser ring and passes through its divergent passages which cause most of the remaining velocity energy to be converted also into pressure and temperature.

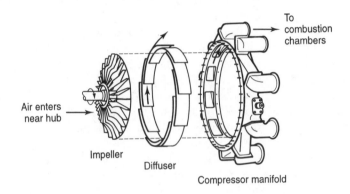

Owing to the high speed of rotation and the two drastic changes in airflow direction, the temperature rise is high. This tends to lower this type of compressor's efficiency. Furthermore, when impeller tip speeds reach sonic values no further pressure rise is possible and this limits the compression ratio to some 4.5:1.

In spite of the adoption of the axial flow type in larger power-plants, some engines still retain the centrifugal compressor because it is simple and comparatively cheap, robust in construction, less vulnerable to damage and less prone to stall and surge. Its main disadvantages are high speed of rotation, large frontal area, limited compression ratio and high temperature rise.

AXIAL-FLOW COMPRESSORS

In this type, many stages of moving and stationary blades are needed. These are positioned alternately so that each row of rotating blades, ROTORS, is followed by a row of stationary vanes, STATORS. One row of rotors and one row of stators is known as one stage.

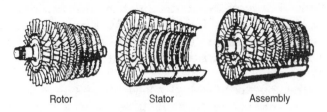

Rotor   Stator   Assembly

Axial flow compressor rotor and stator assembly

Because the air leaving each stage is at a higher pressure, it occupies a smaller space. Therefore each stage of the compressor is smaller than the preceding one and giving the casing a convergent passage. This maintains uniform axial velocity.

Both rotors and stators are of aerofoil section, and between each adjacent rotor and stator the cross-sectional area is divergent.

During rotation the rotors act in a similar manner to a propeller blade and accelerate the air rearward, imparting velocity energy to the air. Because of the divergence some of the velocity energy is converted into pressure and temperature. Leaving the rotors, the air passes across the stators and the divergence here causes the remaining velocity energy to be converted into pressure and temperature. The stators are angled so as to pass the air on to the next set of rotors at the correct angle of attack. Each stage will increase the pressure by some 1.2:1, and the temperature by approximately 25°C.

COMPRESSOR STALL AND SURGE

As the rotors and stators are of aerofoil section the airflow reacts in a similar way to the airflow over a rotor blade. The air must pass over the rotors and stators at the correct angle, otherwise they will cause the flow to become turbulent and stalling will take place.

The angle at which the airflow strikes the blades depends upon the rotational speed and the rate of linear flow, therefore, an axial-flow compressor can only be designed to have these correct flows at one particular RPM and mass flow. Below this RPM, or above it, the angles are incorrect. These types of compressors are designed to be most efficient at the engine's maximum cruise RPM.

Limitation of the maximum engine RPM to a little above this prevents stall at the higher RPM range. Stalling is always possible during acceleration up to cruise, so some control of the airflow below the designed RPM is usually necessary. If stalling becomes excessive the mass flow leaving the compressor is greatly reduced.

As 75% or so of this air is used to keep combustion chamber temperature within limits, it is easy to overheat the system. If combustion pressure also increases owing to the high temperature above the reduced compressor outlet pressure, the airflow will reverse in direction and surge forwards through the compressor, possibly damaging the engine.

A compressor stall can be recognised by the following: vibration, rumbling noise, inability of the engine to accelerate. A compressor surge causes a 'banging' within the intake. All of these symptoms will be accompanied by a rapid rise in temperature.

AIRFLOW CONTROL

To reduce the turbulence of the airflow outside the narrow design range of the compressor, the following devices are fitted to axial-flow compressors:
a) Acceleration control units (fuel system)
b) Inlet guide vanes (fixed or variable)
c) Bleed valves
d) Parallel rear stages (zero stages)
Not all of these devices will necessarily be fitted to all compressors. However, all will have at least inlet guide vanes and an acceleration control unit.

Because the stall problem is greatly increased by the number of stages beyond seven, TWIN SPOOLING was introduced. For example, if fourteen stages of compression are required, this is achieved by two compressors each of seven stages. The airflow leaving the first compressor is straightened and smoothed before entering the second.

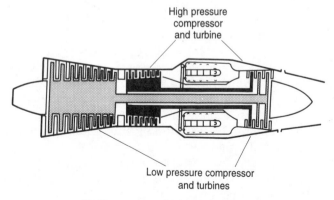

High pressure
compressor
and turbine

Low pressure compressor
and turbines

Turbine arrangement in a twin-spool turbojet

SERVICING OF COMPRESSORS

Little servicing is required on compressors apart from adjustment of the rate of acceleration. However, axial-flow types in particular are vulnerable to damage, so frequent inspection of the blades is necessary. Dirt building up on the blades will reduce efficiency, so compressor washing is carried out at set intervals. A spray of water/kerosene is normally used.

TURBINE ASSEMBLIES

Two basic types of turbine are used to produce torque, the IMPULSE type which utilises the velocity (kinetic energy) of a moving airstream and the REACTION type using the pressure energy in the airstream. Those used in gas turbine engines combine both and are referred to as IMPULSE/REACTION TURBINES.

Ahead of each turbine wheel is placed a set of nozzle guide vanes. These are used to accelerate the gas stream to as high a figure as possible and to direct the gas at the most efficient angle of attack. They have a convergent cross-sectional area between each vane.

TURBINES

A turbine consists of a disc on which is formed or mounted a number of blades. Between each blade a convergent cross-sectional area is formed. Torque is produced by the gas impinging on the blade and/or accelerating through the blade.

The impulse reaction turbine will extract energy from the heat, velocity and pressure energies of the gas stream. As heat energy is the most important, the higher the inlet temperature to the turbine, the greater will be its efficiency. This is of course limited by the materials.

The blades of an impulse/reaction turbine are of aerofoil section with a 'cup shape' at either the forward part of the blade or at the root. This cup shape is the impulse section and in short blades is formed at the forward section of the blade. With long blades the impulse section is formed at the root or base of the blade. The cup or impulse section uses the velocity energy in the stream. The aerofoil reaction section uses the pressure energy to force the gas through the convergence and in both cases heat energy is used up.

TURBINE ASSEMBLIES

A turbine assembly in its simplest form consists of a set of nozzle guide vanes followed by a turbine wheel. This is known as a SINGLE STAGE assembly. To extract more torque an assembly of this type must have the inlet temperature increased, its diameter enlarged, or its RPM increased.

In each case a limit is imposed by the materials used and one way to overcome this limit is by having multi-stage turbines – wheels of smaller diameter in tandem. This allows increased RPM without increased centrifugal loads as well as higher working temperatures.

Up to three stages are normally used. The first stage is the High Pressure (HP) stage, the second is the Intermediate stage and the third the Low Pressure (LP) stage. Where only two stages are used they are the HP and LP stages.

A further advance in temperature increase has been achieved by blade cooling. A percentage of the mass flow is passed through holes formed in the blades. This reduces the blade surface temperature, thereby allowing the inlet temperature to be increased without affecting the material.

A one-, two- or three-stage assembly can be used as a drive for the different sections of the engine, the compressors, the fan or the power take-off to drive propellers, rotors, etc., so some modern engines have three turbine assemblies with possibly a total of six or seven turbines. Each of these assemblies is identified by its position in relation to the combustion chamber outlet – first is the HP assembly, second is the intermediate, and finally the LP assembly.

SERVICING

Servicing of turbines, like compressors, is limited to inspection. All turbine assemblies suffer from 'creep' and are seriously damaged by overheating. Signs of overheating are blade discolouration, blade distortion, cracking, flaking, and reduced tip clearance.

COMBUSTION SYSTEMS

The combustion system is designed to burn fuel as efficiently as possible over the whole range of engine operating conditions. It must do so without any increase in pressure; all the energy released by the fuel is converted into heat and velocity energy.

Very high temperatures exist in the combustion system, the burning temperature of the fuel being around 2,000°C. To protect the materials from which the system is manufactured, a large proportion of the airflow (70%) is used for cooling.

AIRFLOW

The airflow leaving the compressor is first split into two, approximately 25-30% being used for combustion, the other 70-75% being further divided, the greater proportion being used for gas cooling. These three airflows are known as:
a) PRIMARY airflow, for mixing with the fuel and to support combustion
b) SECONDARY airflow, to shape the flame and complete combustion
c) TERTIARY airflow, to cut off the flame and reduce gas temperature to a figure acceptable to the turbine
Secondary and tertiary air also forms a boundary flow on the inside and outside of the flame tube, which is positioned within the air casing. The flame tube is manufactured from special heat resistant steel (Nimonic). The casing is normally mild steel.

TYPES OF SYSTEM

There are basically three types of combustion systems:
a) multiple chamber
b) turbo-annular
c) annular
Type (a) has a number of interconnected chambers in a circle around the spine of the engine. Except for fuel drains and igniters, each chamber is identical on any particular mark of engine.
Type (b) is the 'halfway house' in design between the separate chambers of the multiple and the single chamber of the annular type. It has an annular air casing around the engine spine and indi-

vidual flame tubes fitted within the casing.

Type (c) is a single chamber surrounding the engine. Annular inner and outer casings form a tunnel around the spine of the engine. In the space between the inner and outer casings is fitted an inner and outer flame tube.

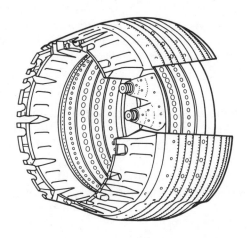

An example of an annular combustion chamber

The three designs can be summed up simply by saying that the multiple type was used on early engines and, although somewhat bulky, it was simple to dismantle and service. The turbo-annular has some of the advantages of the multiple but is more compact and has a smooth exterior and reduced weight and was used on later engines. The annular system, as used on the latest engines, provides a much more compact system and, for the same power output and mass flow, a much shorter one.

EXHAUST SYSTEMS

The design of the exhaust system depends on the use to which the engine is put. Where all the energy is removed from the gas stream by the turbine, the exhaust is simply a pipe taking the waste gas clear of the airframe. When the exhaust gas is to be used for jet propulsion the exhaust system must be designed to make maximum use of the gas stream energy. If reheat is to be used, the exhaust system becomes a very complicated design.

EXHAUST CONES

In nearly every case the exhaust system starts with an exhaust cone. This has three functions:
a)   to prevent the hot gases from eddying back on to the turbine discs
b)   to determine the exhaust gas velocity into the pipe
c)   to use its support vanes in helping to straighten out the gas flow.

PROPULSION SYSTEM (JET)

In this design, after the exhaust cone is the 'jet pipe', which is a parallel tube to clear the airframe, terminating at a 'propellant nozzle'. This nozzle is of extreme importance, being designed to accelerate the gases to the final velocity, normally just below or at Mach 1.

PROPULSION SYSTEM (JET AND REHEAT)

With the reheat system all the problems of a combustion system have to be considered apart from the reduction of the final temperature. Gas stream velocity must be reduced, particularly in the flame area and the fuel must be burnt without causing a pressure rise, which means fitting a variable nozzle.

The fuel system for the reheat must have similar capabilities to the main engine system, all adding up to a complicated design problem. Fuel consumption of these reheat systems is very high so a great deal of consideration must be given before deciding if reheat is worthwhile. Generally speaking, all exhaust systems are made from high-heat-resistant alloys. Apart from reheat systems, servicing is limited to the checking of clearances and for signs of damage from overheating.

LUBRICATION SYSTEMS

Gas turbine engine lubrication systems contain the same main components as piston engine systems. The main difference is the type of oil used and the method of conveying it to and from the lubricated sections.

Because no heavily loaded plain bearings are used in gas turbine engines, the system requires only sufficient pressure to provide a high flow rate to the bearings. The system is a low pressure/high flow when compared with the high pressure/low flow of the piston engine.

THE PRESSURE SIDE

This is similar to the piston engine in having a pressure pump, pressure filter, relief valve and possibly a check valve. Owing to the turbulent nature of a gas turbine engine, instead of oil being passed to the bearings by passages and galleries, internal and external pipes are used.

THE SCAVENGE SIDE

Although the scavenge side is also similar to that of the piston engine, no central pump can be used and internal/external pipes are common. However, because of the method of air sealing and cooling of the bearings, the return oil contains large amounts of air.

To deal with this increased volume, more than one scavenge pump is normally required. The normal de-aerator in the oil tank is insufficient to separate all of this air, so in many cases a centrifugal breather is incorporated in a much larger de-aerator system.

OIL

Because some of the gas turbine engine bearings run in areas of very high temperatures normal oil would tend to carbonise, so a special synthetic oil is used which is able to withstand high temperatures but not very high pressure loads.

SERVICING

Again, very similar to piston engines – cleaning and examination of filters, checking for leaks, etc., and replenishment. The amount of oil used by gas turbine engines is comparatively small, being in pints rather than gallons.

COOLING, AIR SEALING AND HEATING SYSTEMS

All the cooling of gas turbine engines is done by air. Large proportions of the mass flow are used for this purpose but very little of it is wasted from the mass flow thrust calculation. Having been used as a cooling agent, it is passed back into the normal gas flow.

INTAKES AND GUIDE VANES

The intakes normally have hot air passed around a double skin, while the inlet guide vanes are hollow to prevent icing.

NOZZLE GUIDE VANES

Compressor outlet air, part of the tertiary flow, passes through the hollow nozzle guide vanes to join the main gas flow.

TURBINE DISC AND BLADES

Compressor outlet air is again used for cooling of the turbines, being directed up the faces of the discs to prevent the hot gases from seeping down between them. Passages formed by the turbine blades also allow this air to pass through the blades on the more modern high-performance engines.

GENERAL DE-ICING AND HEATING

Other parts of the engine and airframe can be heated by hot air ducted from various parts of the engine either to prevent ice formation or, in some cases, for pressurisation purposes, e.g. fuel tanks. On multi-stage compressors the air is tapped from a section where the air characteristics are the most suitable for the task.

SEALING

Contact seals are rarely used to prevent oil loss from bearings in gas turbine engines. This is because the high RPM would quickly wear them out. Seals which form a series of grooves around a shaft, not in actual contact, are fed with pressure air in the direction opposing oil flow, forming a barrier of air cells at increasing pressure.

SERVICING

Little or no servicing is required for cooling and sealing systems.

SUMMARY OF GAS TURBINES

THE ADVANTAGES OF GAS TURBINES OVER PISTON ENGINES

Fewer moving parts: The gas turbine engine has only one main rotating assembly, whereas a piston engine has many moving parts.
Equal power for less weight: For equal power a gas turbine can be as little as half the weight of a piston engine.
More efficient: A piston engine is about 20-30% efficient, whereas a gas turbine engine is about 40-50% efficient.
Less servicing: As a gas turbine engine has fewer moving parts, its maintenance requirement is less.
Better operating range: The gas turbine's efficiency increases with altitude. The reverse is true of a piston engine.
Constant moving airflow: The airflow through a gas turbine engine is continuous, whereas the airflow through a piston engine is drawn in, stopped, does its work and then is moved on again. Having a continuous airflow means greater power is available, because a greater mass of combustion is passed through the engine.

THE DISADVANTAGE OF GAS TURBINES COMPARED WITH PISTON ENGINES

High cost: A gas turbine costs a great deal more than a piston engine, although this extra cost is balanced out by its advantages.
Fragile: A gas turbine engine is far less robust than a piston engine and requires better work and dispersal area husbandry to prevent the ingestion of foreign bodies, causing foreign object damage (FOD).
Greater engineering requirements: This disadvantage goes hand in hand with cost. The construction problems of compressors and turbines result in high costs in time and labour.
Running problems: A gas turbine tends to be a constant-speed engine owing to the size of the rotating assembly. Whether constant speed or not, the running temperatures are critical. Overfuelling results in surging which causes vibrations and damage to bearings, blades, etc. Ingestion causes damage to the first-stage compressor which will cause further damage to the engine as the foreign object damage, plus compressor blade(s), flow through the remainder of the engine.

TYPES OF GAS TURBINE ENGINES

Fixed Spool

Characteristics: The turbine and compressors are directly linked. This type of engine varies power output by varying the amount of fuel in the combustion chamber to vary the force applied to the turbine. The engine is constant speed.

Advantages: Simple design; few moving parts; governor-controlled fuel system because the engine is constant speed.

Free Turbine

Characteristics: A set of turbines is linked to compressors to rotate them and, together with the combustion chamber, is known as a GAS GENERATOR. An independent turbine, free of this first shaft, is linked to the propeller or main rotor. Within a large range of free turbine rotational speed the power varies just a little, i.e. the efficiency of the free turbine is not greatly influenced by its rotational speed. The best conditions for achieving maximum power are present when the rotational speed of the free turbine is as low as that of the gas generator.

The torque on the transmission shaft varies inversely with the free turbine's rotational speed. Torque reaches maximum when the free turbine speed is zero and the gas generator is operating at maximum RPM.

Advantages: Easy starting; no need to have a clutch fitted; power demands are better met because the gas generator works independently.

Multi-Spool

Characteristics: A spool is a shaft with a compressor on one end and a turbine on the other. A multi-spool turbo-jet consists of more than one spool, each spool being independent of the other, although coaxial.

In a twin-spool gas generator the first-stage compressor and the last-stage turbine make an LP spool and the second-stage compressor and the first-stage turbine make an HP spool.

Multi-spool is best suited to bypass turbojets. In a bypass engine the LP compressor provides additional air, some of which is passed outside the gas generator, to be added to the exhaust airstream to improve efficiency and provide extra thrust.

Advantages: Reduced risk of surge at altitude; greater efficiency; compression rates indentical to those of a fixed spool but with fewer compressor stages; driving the LP and HP compressors at different RPMs without the use of reduction gears; with the HP turbine being rotated at a faster RPM than the LP, the safety temperature and RPM range for 'creep' is greater – this allows higher expansion rates and a reduction in the number of turbine stages; a reduction in weight and length of the engine; ease of starting.

Multi-Spool (Free Turbine)

Characteristics: Those of the multi-spool and also those of the free turbine. The free turbine drive to the propeller or main rotor may either be taken externally through gearboxes and driveshafts or pass through the engine in the form of a spool, but passes out the front of the engine to drive either the propeller or the main rotor.

Advantages: All those mentioned for the free turbine and multi-spool engines.

SURGE

This phenomenon results from unstable operation of the engine. The limits of the compressor's work rate are set by the combustion chamber, the turbine and the tailpipe.

The pressure at the intake side of the compressor is known as P1. The pressure on the output side of the compressor is P2, and that at the output of the combustion chamber is P3. P4 is the pressure measured after the turbine

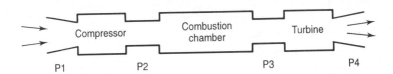

If, for reasons which we shall look into, the pressure at P3 becomes greater than that at P2, the compressor airflow stops and the expansion takes place towards the compressor as well as the turbine. Being no longer supplied with air P3 falls, the compressor starts working again until the downstream pressure overtakes the discharge, and so on. This cyclical phenomenon occurs at a rate of about 120 cycles per second, and clearly disturbs the working of the engine and has serious effects. Surging occurs every time P3 becomes greater than P2. It can be due to an excessive fall of P2 (upstream circuit), or to an excessive increase of P3 (downstream circuit).

A distinction can be made between surging coming from the upstream circuit or the downstream one.

Upstream circuit: A disturbance in the airflow will cause an aerodynamic stall on the compressor blades, resulting in a fall in P2 and bringing on a surge. Any deterioration or defect in the air intake and the compressor could therefore result in surging. An identical phenomenon may also occur when the speed of sound is achieved at any point on the compressor.

Downstream circuit: When the pressure in the downstream circuit becomes too great, or rises suddenly, surging may occur. The main causes are too sudden a change in the rate, or defect or deterioration in the combustion chamber, the turbine or the exhaust system. The consequences of surging are:

a) increase in temperature at the turbine entry which could lead to deterioration of the turbine

b) heavy vibrations which could lead to deterioration of the rotating assembly and the bearings

c) abnormal and violent noises

d) smoke and flames

The recommended procedures and remedies:

a) in a turbojet the fuel flow should be reduced and the aircraft put into a dive

b) in a turboprop the load put on the gas generator by the receiving body should be reduced (reduce propeller RPM).

After surging the engine should be inspected. Some devices available to prevent surging are discharge valves, air intake guide vanes and acceleration control units.

THE ALLISON 250 SERIES TURBOSHAFT ENGINE

INTRODUCTION

The Allison 250 series turboshaft engine is an internal combustion gas turbine engine featuring a 'free' power turbine. The engine consists of a combination axial-centrifugal compressor; a single 'can' type combustor; a turbine assembly which incorporates a two-stage gas producer turbine, a two-stage power turbine and an exhaust collector; and an accessory gearbox which incorporates a gas producer gear train and a power turbine gear train. The following definitions apply to this engine:

FRONT: The compressor end of the engine.

REAR: The combustion end of the engine.

TOP: The exhaust gases outlet side of the engine.

BOTTOM: Determined by scavenge oil outlet fittings and burner drain plug.

RIGHT AND LEFT: Determined when standing at the rear of the engine facing forward.

DIRECTION OF ROTATION: Determined when standing at the rear of the engine facing forward. The gas producer turbine and power turbine rotors rotate in a clockwise direction.

ACCESSORIES ROTATION: Determined by facing the accessory mounting pad.

COMPRESSOR STAGE: Consists of a rotor and a stator. The rotor blades accelerate the air into the stator vanes. The vanes decrease the velocity and increase the static pressure of the air.

TURBINE STAGE: Consists of a stator and a rotor. The stator vanes accelerate the exhaust gases into the rotor blades, which then absorb the energy from the gas.

COMPRESSOR AND TURBINE STAGES NUMBERING: Numbered in direction of airflow. The compressor axial stages are numbered one through to six, with the first stage at the front and the sixth stage at the rear. The turbine rotor stages are numbered one through to four with the first stage at the rear and the fourth stage at the front.

MAIN BEARINGS NUMBERING: Numbered one through to eight in a front-to-rear direction. Compressor rotor bearings are nos. 1 and 2; the spur adapter gear shaft bearing is no 2½; helical power train drive (pinion) gear bearings are nos. 3 and 4; power turbine rotor bearings are nos. 7 and 8. There are a total of nine main bearings.

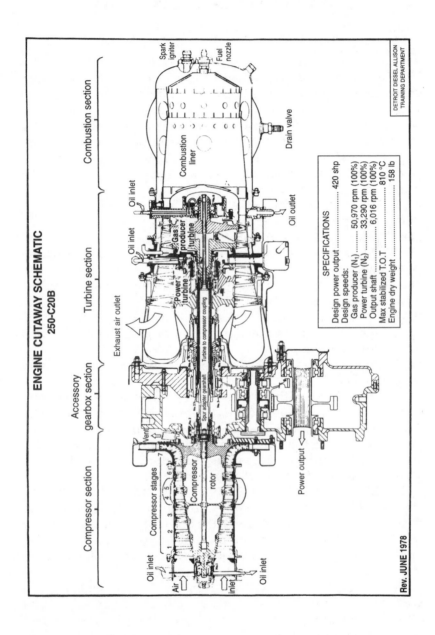

ENGINE CUTAWAY SCHEMATIC
250-C20B

Compressor section

Accessory gearbox section

Turbine section

Combustion section

Spark igniter

Fuel nozzle

Oil inlet

Oil inlet

Oil inlet

Oil inlet

Gas producer turbine

Power turbine

Combustion liner

Drain valve

Oil outlet

Exhaust air outlet

Turbine to compressor coupling

Spur adapter gearshaft

Power output

Vent

7 6 5 4 3 2 1

Compressor stages

Compressor rotor

Oil inlet

Air inlet

Oil inlet

SPECIFICATIONS

Design power output. .... 420 shp
Design speeds:
Gas producer (N_1) .... 50,970 rpm (100%)
Power turbine (N_2) .... 33,290 rpm (100%)
Output shaft .... 6,016 rpm (100%)
Max stabilized T.O.T. .... 810 °C
Engine dry weight .... 158 lb

DETROIT DIESEL ALLISON
TRAINING DEPARTMENT

Rev. JUNE 1978

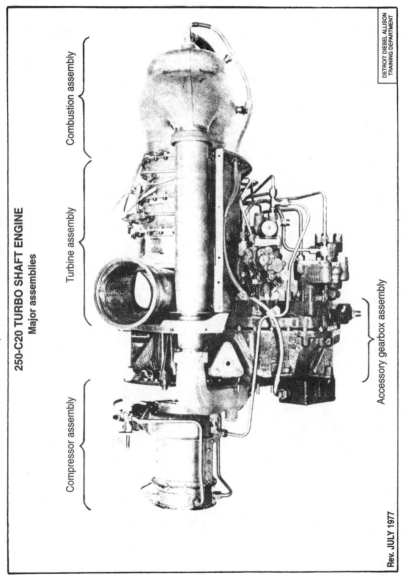

Helicop. Pilots Manual V.2 Relet 2 60%

250-C20 TURBO SHAFT ENGINE
Major assemblies

Combustion assembly

Turbine assembly

Compressor assembly

Accessory gearbox assembly

DETROIT DIESEL ALLISON
TRAINING DEPARTMENT

Rev. JULY 1977

Performance ratings standard static sea level conditions

Model 250-C20B ratings	Output shp (min)	N₁ gas producer rpm (est.)	Output shaft rpm	Power turbine rpm	S.F.C lb/hr/shp (max)	F.F. fuel flow lbs/hr (max)	RAM power rating at output shaft Torque ft-lbs (max)	RAM power rating at output shaft S.H.P. (max)	T.O.T measured rated gas temperature °F	T.O.T measured rated gas temperature °C	Net jet thrust lbs (min)
Takeoff (5 min) *30-minute power	420	53,000 104%	6,016 100%	33,290 100%	0.650	273	384	439.8	1490	810	42
*Max. continuous	420	53,000 104%	6,016 100%	33,290 100%	0.650	273	384	439.8	1490	810	42
Normal cruise	370	51,200 100.4%	6,016 100%	33,290 100%	0.650	240	323	369.9	1360	738	38
Cruise A (90%)	333	50,160 98.4%	6,016 100%	33,290 100%	0.665	221	323	369.9	1286	697	36
Cruise B (75%)	278	48,800 95.5%	6,016 100%	33,290 100%	0.709	197	323	369.9	1197	647	32
Ground idle	35 max.	33,000 64.7%	4500-75% to 6300-105%	24,968-75% to 34,950-105%	—	70	—	—	800 ±100	427 ±38	10
Flight autorotation	0	33,000 64.7%	5900-98% to 6480-106%	32,725-98% to 35,280-106%	—	70	—	—	775 ±100	402 ±38	10

*This rating is applicable only during one-engine-out operation of multi-engined aircraft

$100\%\ N_1 = 50,970$ rpm
$100\%\ N_2 = 33,290$ rpm

T.O.T = gas producer turbine outlet temperature
F.F. = fuel flow
S.H.P. = shaft horsepower
S.F.C. = specific fuel consumption

$$S.F.C. = \frac{F.F.}{S.H.P.} \quad \text{thus, takeoff } S.F.C. = \frac{273\ lbs/hr}{420\ shp} = 0.650\ lbs/hr/shp$$

$$S.H.P. = \frac{torque \times N_2 \times 0.18071}{5252} = \frac{384 \times 6016}{5252} \quad \text{where torque is in ft/lbs \& } N_2 \text{ is power turbine rpm}$$

$$\text{thus takeoff RAM power rating shp} = \frac{384 \times 6016}{5252} = 439.4$$

JAN. 1984

Allison
TURBINE SCHOOL

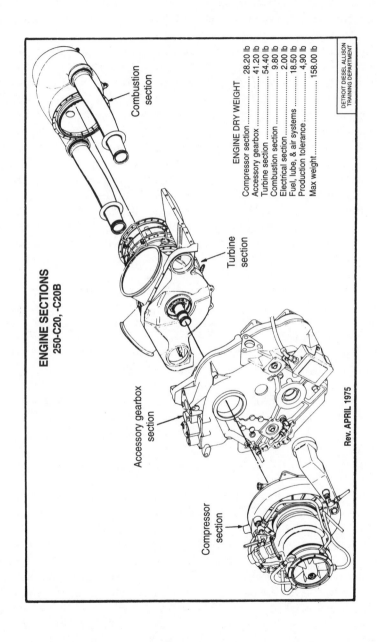

ENGINE SECTIONS
250-C20, -C20B

Combustion section

Turbine section

Accessory gearbox section

Compressor section

ENGINE DRY WEIGHT

Compressor section	28.20 lb
Accessory gearbox	41.20 lb
Turbine section	54.40 lb
Combustion section	9.80 lb
Electrical section	2.00 lb
Fuel, lube, & air systems	18.50 lb
Production tolerance	4.90 lb
Max weight	158.00 lb

DETROIT DIESEL ALLISON
TRAINING DEPARTMENT

Rev. APRIL 1975

COMPRESSOR ASSEMBLY

The compressor assembly consists of a compressor, front support assembly, compressor rotor assembly, compressor case assembly and a compressor diffuser assembly.

The front support assembly, fabricated from stainless steel, has seven hollow radial struts brazed to a double wall outer skin and a double wall hub. The struts are designed to direct and distribute air into the compressor rotor in an efficient manner. Operation of the engine in icing conditions can result in undesirable ice formations on the compressor front support, therefore the engine is equipped with a hot-air type anti-icing system. If icing conditions are encountered, the pilot activates the system and hot compressor discharge air is directed to two ports on the compressor front support. Hot air flows between the walls of the outer skin into hollow radial struts, through the struts, and between the walls of the hub. Anti-icing air is exhausted out of slots on the trailing edges of the struts and out of holes in the hub. The flow of hot anti-icing air keeps the temperature of the compressor front support above the freezing point of water and, thus, the engine is 'anti-iced'.

The compressor rotor front (no. 1) bearing is housed and supported in the compressor front support. Pressure oil for lubrication is delivered to the no. 1 bearing through a tube in the upper strut of the compressor front support. Oil is scavenged from the compressor front support through a tube in the bottom strut. A spring-loaded carbon seal is used to prevent oil leakage from the compressor front support.

The compressor rotor assembly is a combination axial-centrifugal type with six axial stages and one centrifugal stage. The axial stages are precision-cast combination wheel and blade assemblies, and the centrifugal stage consists of a precision-cast impeller. The wheel and blade assemblies and the impeller are made from stainless steel. The no. 1 bearing is housed in the compressor front support and the no. 2 bearing is housed in the compressor rear diffuser. The no. 2 bearing serves as the thrust bearing for the compressor rotor assembly.

The compressor case assembly consists of an upper and a lower case. These cases are fabricated from stainless steel and have flanges at the front and rear. The constant-diameter case assembly houses and retains the cantilever designed compressor vane assemblies. Thermal-setting plastic is centrifugally cast to the inside surface of the case halves and vane outer bands. To have good compressor efficiency it is necessary to have minimum clearance

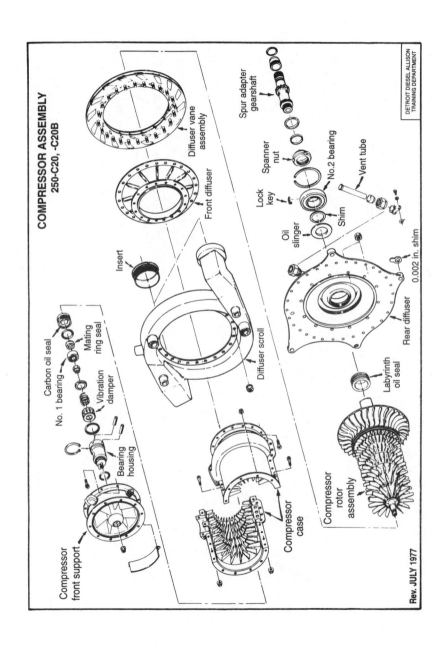

COMPRESSOR ASSEMBLY
250-C20, -C20B

Diffuser vane assembly

Front diffuser

Spur adapter gearshaft

Spanner nut

No.2 bearing

Vent tube

Lock key

Shim

Oil slinger

0.002 in. shim

Rear diffuser

Insert

Carbon oil seal

Mating ring seal

No. 1 bearing

Vibration damper

Bearing housing

Diffuser scroll

Compressor front support

Labyrinth oil seal

Compressor rotor assembly

Compressor case

DETROIT DIESEL ALLISON
TRAINING DEPARTMENT

Rev. JULY 1977

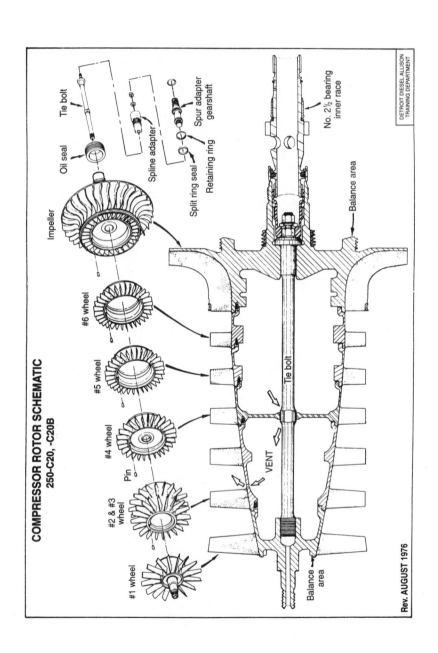

COMPRESSOR ROTOR SCHEMATIC
250-C20, -C20B

Tie bolt

Oil seal

Spline adapter

Spur adapter gearshaft

Split ring seal

Retaining ring

Impeller

No. 2½ bearing inner race

Balance area

Tie bolt

VENT

Balance area

#1 wheel

#2 & #3 wheel

Pin

#4 wheel

#5 wheel

#6 wheel

DETROIT DIESEL ALLISON TRAINING DEPARTMENT

Rev. AUGUST 1976

116

between the rotor blade tips and the case. The use of plastic in the case provides for minimum rotor blade tip clearance. If the blade tips contact the plastic then the plastic will be abraded or worn away without damage to either the case or the blades. For the engine to have good acceleration characteristics it is necessary to bleed air off the compressor at lower compressor ratios. The compressor case assembly has provisions for mounting a bleed-air control valve which bleeds air off the fifth stage of the compressor during starting and all engine operation at low pressure ratios.

The compressor diffuser assembly consists of stainless steel front and rear diffusers, a diffuser scroll and a diffuser vane assembly. The compressor rotor impeller is housed within the diffuser assembly. For good efficiency there must be minimum impeller front face clearance, so aluminium is sprayed on to the contoured front diffuser. If the impeller should make contact, the aluminium will be abraded or worn away without damage to either the front diffuser or the impeller. The diffuser vane assembly has vanes which direct air from the impeller into the diffuser scroll, which then delivers it into two 'elbows'. Each elbow contains stainless steel turning vanes which redirect the airflow from an outward to a rearward direction. Compressor discharge air tubes deliver compressed air from the outlet of the elbows to the combustion outer case. The diffuser scroll has five ports from which air can be bled or compressor discharge air pressure sensed.

COMBUSTION ASSEMBLY

The combustion assembly comprises the combustion outer case and a combustion liner. The outer case is a fabricated stainless steel part with provision for mounting a burner drain valve, a fuel nozzle and a spark igniter. The combustion liner must provide for rapid mixing of fuel and air and it must control the flame length and position such that the flame does not contact any metallic surface.

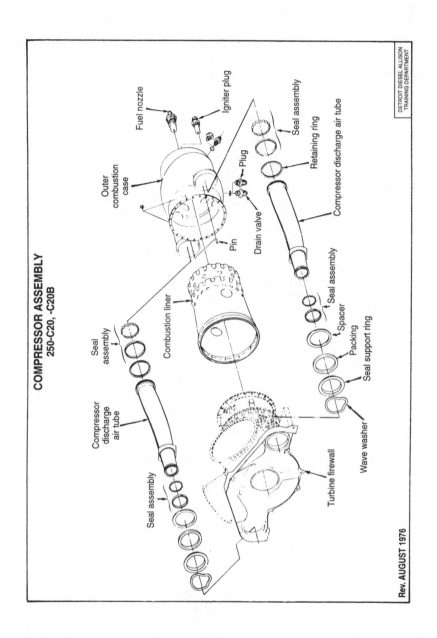

COMPRESSOR ASSEMBLY
250-C20, -C20B

Fuel nozzle
Igniter plug
Outer combustion case
Pin
Plug
Drain valve
Seal assembly
Retaining ring
Compressor discharge air tube
Seal assembly
Spacer
Packing
Seal support ring
Wave washer
Turbine firewall
Seal assembly
Seal assembly
Combustion liner
Compressor discharge air tube

DETROIT DIESEL ALLISON
TRAINING DEPARTMENT

Rev. AUGUST 1976

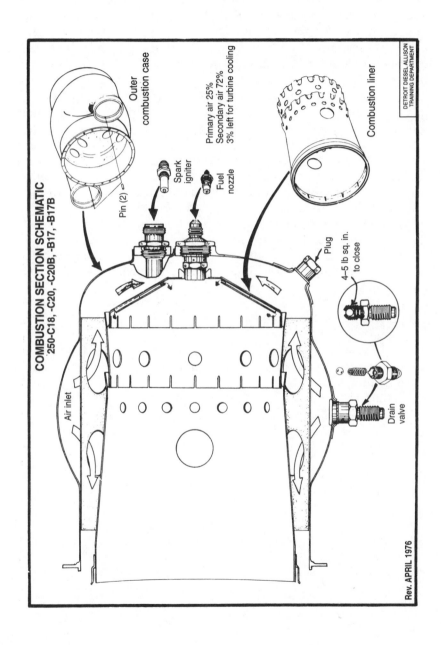

COMBUSTION SECTION SCHEMATIC
250-C18, -C20, -C20B, -B17, -B17B

Outer combustion case

Pin (2)

Spark igniter

Fuel nozzle

Primary air 25%
Secondary air 72%
3% left for turbine cooling

Combustion liner

Air inlet

Plug

4–5 lb sq. in. to close

Drain valve

DETROIT DIESEL ALLISON
TRAINING DEPARTMENT

Rev. APRIL 1976

119

TURBINE ASSEMBLY

The turbine assembly of the engine is that part incorporating the components necessary for the development of power and the exhausting of gases. The turbine assembly has a two-stage gas producer turbine and a two-stage power turbine. Power to drive the compressor rotor is furnished by the gas producer turbine rotor through a direct drive. The power turbine rotor converts the remaining gas energy into power which is delivered to the power output pads of the engine. Exhausting gases from the power turbine are directed into the exhaust collector support, which provides for exhaust flow through two elliptical ducts at the top of the engine. These ducts are 40° on either side of the top centreline.

The gas producer turbine consists of the first and second turbine stages and the power turbine consists of the third and fourth turbine stages. The gas producer and power turbine rotors are not mechanically coupled but gas coupled, in that the exhausting gases must flow through the four turbine stages. The power turbine is a 'free turbine' since it is free to rotate at a different speed than the gas producer turbine rotor. The free power turbine design has the following advantages:

a) added operational flexibility, for there is the freedom of independent selection of gas producer rotor and power turbine rotor speeds

b) improvement of overall engine performance because each turbine can be designed for maximum efficiency at its primary operating point

c) facilitates engine starts in that the starter does not have to crank the power turbine and helicopter rotor system

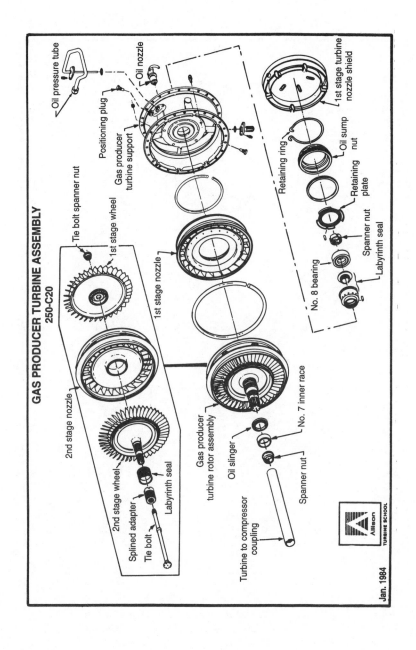

GAS PRODUCER TURBINE ASSEMBLY
250-C20

Oil pressure tube
Oil nozzle
Positioning plug
Tie bolt spanner nut
Gas producer turbine support
1st stage wheel
1st stage turbine nozzle shield
Retaining ring
Oil sump nut
Retaining plate
Spanner nut
Labyrinth seal
No. 8 bearing
1st stage nozzle
2nd stage nozzle
2nd stage wheel
Splined adapter
Tie bolt
Labyrinth seal
Gas producer turbine rotor assembly
Oil slinger
No. 7 inner race
Spanner nut
Turbine to compressor coupling

Jan. 1984

Allison
TURBINE SCHOOL

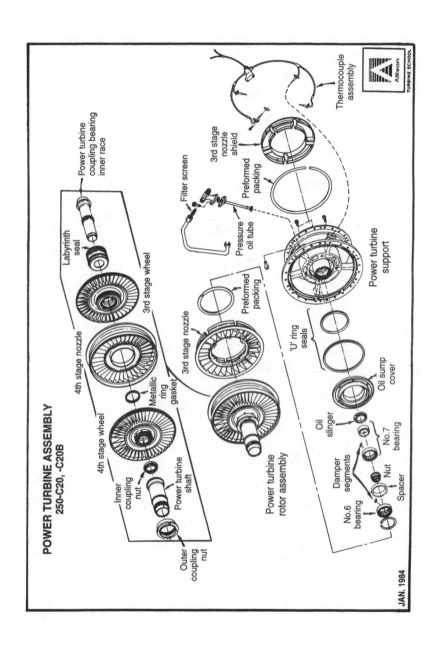

POWER TURBINE ASSEMBLY
250-C20, -C20B

Power turbine coupling bearing inner race

Labyrinth seal

3rd stage wheel

4th stage nozzle

4th stage wheel

Inner coupling nut

Power turbine shaft

Metallic ring gasket

3rd stage nozzle

Outer coupling nut

Filter screen

3rd stage nozzle shield

Preformed packing

Pressure oil tube

Power turbine support

Preformed packing

'U' ring seals

Oil sump cover

Oil slinger

No.7 bearing

Damper segments

Nut

Spacer

No.6 bearing

Power turbine rotor assembly

Thermocouple assembly

Allison TURBINE SCHOOL

JAN. 1984

122

ACCESSORY GEARBOX ASSEMBLY

The accessory gearbox is the primary structural member of the engine as it provides mounting and support for the compressor and turbine assemblies. The gearbox housing, which is the most rigid structural member of the engine, has four engine mounting pads.

The accessory gearbox contains most of the lubrication system components and incorporates two separate gear trains. The purpose of the power turbine gear train is to reduce the engine speed from 33,290 RPM at the power turbine rotor to 6,016 RPM at the power output pads. It also incorporates a torque-meter to measure engine output torque. The power turbine tachometer generator and power turbine governor are driven by the power turbine gear train. The gas producer gear train provides drive for the oil pumps, fuel pump, gas producer fuel control, gas producer tachometer generator and starter-generator. During starting the starter-generator cranks the engine through the gas producer gear train.

The oil pump assembly, which incorporates a pressure element and four scavenge elements, is mounted within the gearbox and on the housing. An oil filter assembly is mounted on and extends into the top of the housing. Pressure oil is filtered and then delivered to oil transfer ports and to oil nozzles within the gearbox. Scavenge elements of the oil pump assembly scavenge oil from the compressor front support, gas producer turbine support, power turbine support and gearbox sumps.

The helicopter manufacturer provides the oil tank, oil cooler and all lines which connect the engine lubrication system to the helicopter supply system. The oil tank is vented to the interior of the gearbox and the gearbox is vented overboard.

The power turbine gear train has helical gears which produce an axial thrust on the torque-meter whenever torque is delivered to the power output gear. The axial thrust is directly proportional to the torque transmitted through the helical gears. Pressure oil delivered to the torque-meter is metered as required to counterbalance the axial thrust. Thus, torque-meter pressure is directly proportional to the output torque.

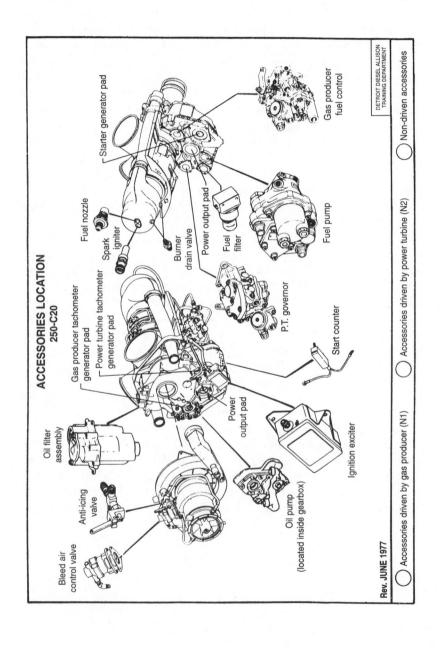

ACCESSORIES LOCATION
250-C20

Rev. JUNE 1977

DETROIT DIESEL ALLISON
TRAINING DEPARTMENT

○ Accessories driven by gas producer (N1) ○ Accessories driven by power turbine (N2) ○ Non-driven accessories

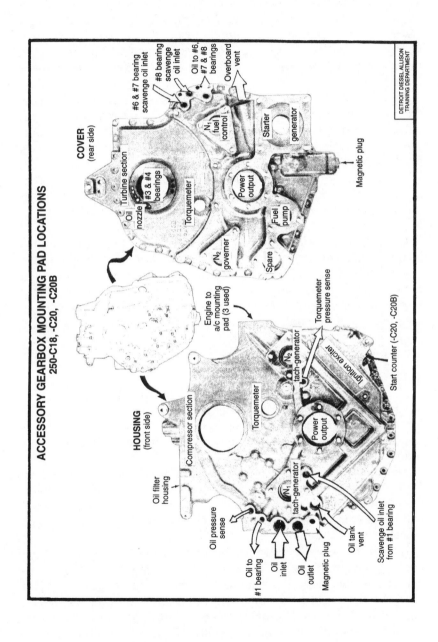

ACCESSORY GEARBOX MOUNTING PAD LOCATIONS
250-C18, -C20, -C20B

COVER (rear side)

#6 & #7 bearing scavenge oil inlet
#8 bearing scavenge oil inlet
Oil to #6, #7 & #8 bearings
Overboard vent
N_1 fuel control
Starter
generator
Magnetic plug
Turbine section
Oil nozzle
#3 & #4 bearings
Torquemeter
Power output
Fuel pump
N_2 governor
Spare

Engine to a/c mounting pad (3 used)

HOUSING (front side)

Torquemeter pressure sense
Start counter (-C20, -C20B)
Ignition exciter
N_2 tach-generator
Torquemeter
Power output
Compressor section
N_1 tach-generator
Oil filter housing
Oil pressure sense
Oil to #1 bearing
Oil inlet
Oil outlet
Magnetic plug
Oil tank vent
Scavenge oil inlet from #1 bearing

DETROIT DIESEL ALLISON TRAINING DEPARTMENT

LUBRICATION SYSTEM

The lubricating system is a circulating dry-sump type with an external oil tank and oil cooler, both of which are mounted and furnished by the helicopter manufacturer. The system is designed to provide adequate lubrication, scavenging and cooling as needed for bearings, splines and gears, regardless of helicopter attitude or altitude.

Jet lubrication is provided to all compressor, gas producer turbine and power turbine rotor bearings and to bearings and gear meshes of the power turbine gear train with the exception of the power output shaft bearings. These and all other gears and bearings are lubricated by oil mist.

An assembly consisting of an oil filter, filter bypass valve and pressure regulating valve is located in the upper right-hand side of the accessory gearbox. A check valve is located in the oil filter outlet passage.

Oil from the tank is delivered to the pressure pump which pumps oil through the oil filter and then to various points of lubrication. The check valve is open when the engine is running and closed when the engine is not in operation. The system oil pressure is regulated by the pressure regulating valve and is at a relatively high value to balance the high axial gear thrust in the torque-meter. This high thrust value is necessary to minimise friction effects and provide accurate measurement of torque.

ANTI-ICING SYSTEM

Operation of the engine during icing conditions could result in ice formations on the compressor front support. If ice were allowed to build up the airflow to the engine would be affected and engine performance reduced.

The anti-icing system includes an anti-icing valve mounted on the front face of the diffuser scroll, two stainless steel lines between the anti-icing valve and the compressor front support and passages within the compressor front support itself. Anti-icing operation must be selected by the pilot.

When the system is in operation, compressor discharge air, which has been heated owing to compression, will flow through the anti-icing valve and tubes to the compressor front support passages. Hot air flows between the double wall outer shell and into the seven hollow radial struts. The hot air flowing through the radial struts exhausts either out of small slots in the trailing edge of the struts or out of the double wall hub of the compressor front support.

COMPRESSOR BLEED AIR SYSTEM

This is an entirely automatic system which bleeds air from the fifth stage of the compressor during engine starting, acceleration and at low compressor pressure ratio operation. It includes a bleed-air control valve attached to the compressor case which bleeds off fifth stage pressure at low pressure ratios to prevent compressor stall and surge.

The compressor blades and vanes are aerofoils. If the angle of attack becomes too great or if the air velocity becomes too low, air-flow separation occurs and the aerofoil stalls. This results in loss of efficiency, a loss of pressure ratio and, therefore, a reduction in pressure level at the compressor outlet. To produce engines with good fuel consumption and rapid acceleration characteristics it is necessary to operate as close as possible to the stall region.

The ability of the compressor to pump air is a function of RPM. At low RPM the compressor does not have the same ability to pump air as it does at higher RPM. To keep the angle of attack and air velocity within the desired limits it is necessary to 'unload' the compressor in some way during starting and low-power operation.

A slot, located at the compressor fifth stage rotor blade, allows an equal bleed of compressor air into a manifold which is an integral part of the compressor case. The air bleed valve is open during starting and ground idle operation and it remains open until a predetermined pressure ratio is obtained, at which time the valve begins to modulate from the open to the closed position.

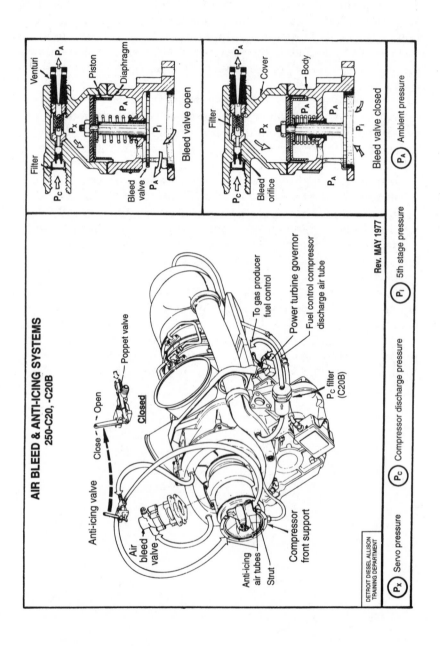

AIR BLEED & ANTI-ICING SYSTEMS
250-C20, -C20B

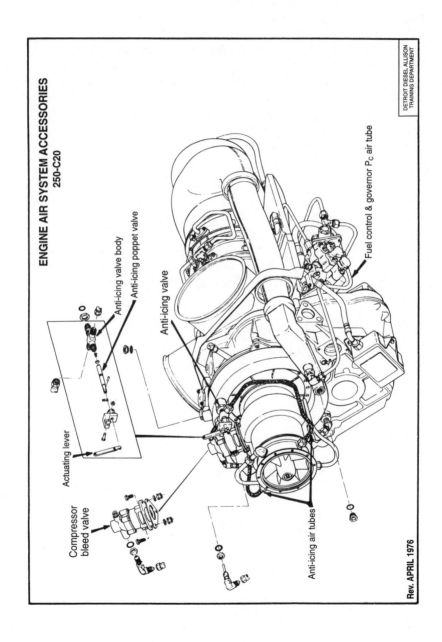

ENGINE AIR SYSTEM ACCESSORIES
250-C20

Anti-icing valve body
Anti-icing poppet valve
Anti-icing valve
Actuating lever
Compressor bleed valve
Anti-icing air tubes
Fuel control & governor P$_c$ air tube

DETROIT DIESEL ALLISON
TRAINING DEPARTMENT

Rev. APRIL 1976

IGNITION SYSTEM

Ignition is only required during starting because the combustion process is continuous. Once ignition takes place, the flame in the combustion liner acts as the ignition agent for the fuel-air mixture.

The ignition system is composed of three basic parts: a low-tension capacitor discharge ignition exciter assembly, a spark igniter lead, and a shunted surface gap spark igniter. This system is powered by the helicopter's 28-V DC electrical system, but will function from a 14- to 30-V DC input.

TEMPERATURE MEASUREMENT SYSTEM

An equal resistance branch thermocouple harness assembly with four integral probes is used to sense the temperature of the gases on the outlet side of the gas producer turbine rotor. Each thermocouple probe consists of a single element chromel-alumel assembly with a bare wire junction. A DC voltage, directly proportional to the gas temperature it senses, is generated by each thermocouple. Together, the thermocouples provide an average of the four voltages representative of the turbine outlet temperature (TOT).

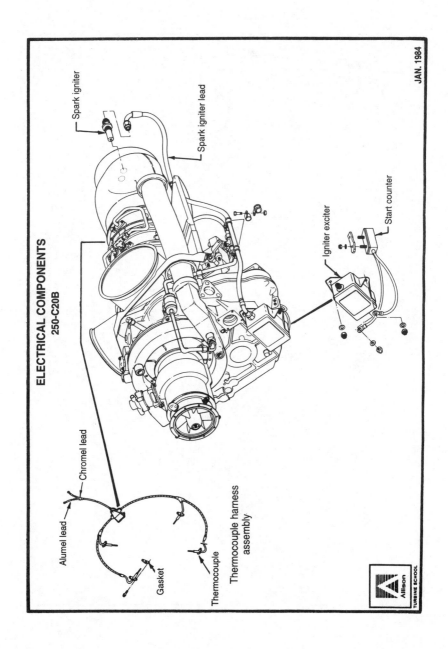

ELECTRICAL COMPONENTS
250-C20B

Spark igniter

Spark igniter lead

Start counter

Igniter exciter

Chromel lead

Alumel lead

Gasket

Thermocouple

Thermocouple harness
assembly

JAN. 1984

Allison
TURBINE SCHOOL

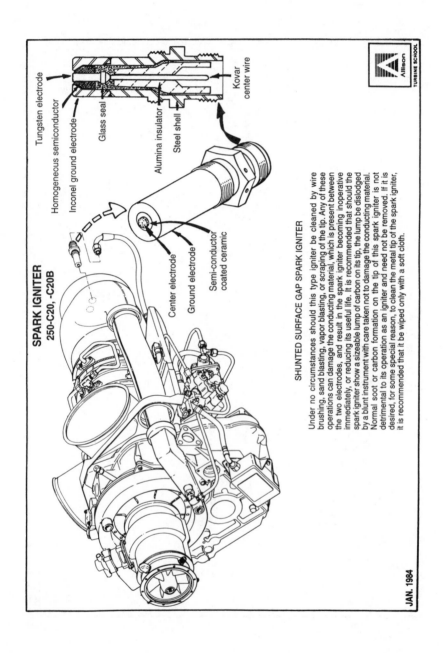

SPARK IGNITER
250-C20, -C20B

Tungsten electrode

Homogeneous semiconductor

Inconel ground electrode

Glass seal

Alumina insulator

Steel shell

Kovar center wire

Center electrode

Ground electrode

Semi-conductor coated ceramic

Allison
TURBINE SCHOOL

JAN. 1984

SHUNTED SURFACE GAP SPARK IGNITER

Under no circumstances should this type igniter be cleaned by wire brushing, sand blasting, vapor blasting, or scraping of the tip. Any of these operations can damage the conducting material, which is present between the two electrodes, and result in the spark igniter becoming inoperative immediately, or reducing its useful life. It is recommended that should the spark igniter show a sizeable lump of carbon on its tip, the lump be dislodged by a blunt instrument with care taken not to damage the conducting material. Normal soot or carbon formation on the tip of this spark igniter is not detrimental to its operation as an igniter and need not be removed. If it is desired, for some special reason, to clean the metal tip of the spark igniter, it is recommended that it be wiped only with a soft cloth.

FUEL SYSTEM

The fuel system includes a fuel pump and filter assembly, a gas producer fuel control, a power turbine governor, a fuel nozzle and a burner drain valve. The engine operates on MIL-T-5624F, Grade JP-4, Jet A1 or other approved alternative fuels. The fuel system must deliver metered fuel to the fuel nozzle to meet all possible conditions of engine operation either on the ground or in flight. This means that the fuel system must:

a) have the capability of starting the engine under all ambient conditions
b) meter fuel to prevent compressor stall and surge
c) meter fuel as a function of gas producer (N1) RPM during starting and ground idle operation
d) meter fuel as a function of power turbine (N2)
e) provide the means of limiting N1 to approximately 104% in the event of power turbine governor malfunction
f) provide a means of stopping fuel flow to the engine

The fuel pump and filter assembly incorporates a bypass valve and a bypass pressure regulating valve (PRV). In the event of fuel contamination, the bypass valve opens to permit fuel flow to the pump. When the engine is operating, the gas producer fuel control bypasses fuel back to the pump assembly with the regulating valve controlling the bypass fuel pressure.

The gas producer fuel control and the power turbine governor provide for a fuel metering system. This system senses gas producer (N1) RPM power turbine (N2) RPM, compressor discharge pressure and throttle position to regulate and maintain fuel flow. The system meets the following requirements:

a) provides speed governing of the power turbine rotor
b) provides overspeed protection for the gas producer rotor system and the power turbine rotor system
c) regulates engine functions during starting, acceleration, governing, deceleration and shutdown

The fuel nozzle has a single entry and a dual outlet orifice and provides a finely atomised spray of fuel at all flow conditions required by the engine. The nozzle is equipped with a filter to minimise the possibility of contamination, and is designed to prevent 'dribbling' of fuel after shutdown.

The burner drain valve is located on the bottom of the combustion outer casing and is spring-loaded to the open position. It is closed when the combustion chamber pressure exceeds a predetermined value and remains closed during all engine operation. On shutdown, a spring opens the valve, thus preventing any accumulation of fuel in the combustion outer casing.

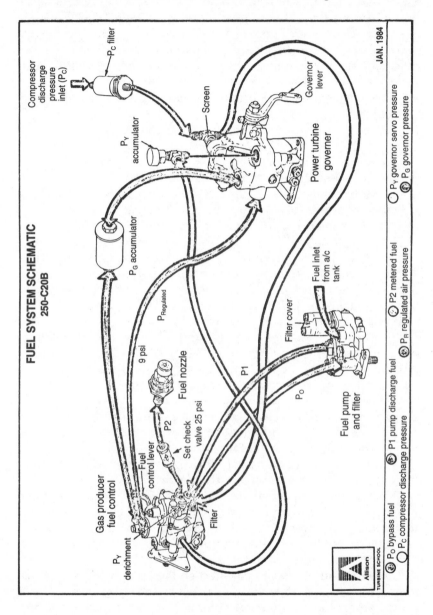

THE FUNDAMENTALS OF THE ALLISON 250 SERIES TURBOSHAFT ENGINE

In this engine the absorption of energy from the gases of combustion and the development of shaft horsepower are accomplished by means of four turbine stages. The turbines provide the means of extracting gas energy and converting it into mechanical energy, therefore this engine is classified as a gas turbine and as such it must have the following operational sections for producing power: intake section, compressor section, combustion section, turbine section, exhaust section.

Intake Section: One of the factors which determines the power being developed by a turbine engine is the weight of air that flows through that engine per unit of time. The intake section must therefore offer minimum restriction to the flow of air and be designed so that ice formation cannot result in a complete blockage of the airflow to the compressor. It must also incorporate some means of preventing the entry of foreign objects which could damage the engine.

Compressor Section: That part of the engine which produces an air pressure rise and comprises six radial stages and one centrifugal stage. The impeller accelerates the air into the scroll which delivers it to two diffusing discharge tubes. The highest total air pressure is at the inlet of the diffuser scroll. As the air passes rearward the velocity decreases and the static pressure increases, with the highest pressure at the inlet to the combustion section.

The compressor rotor can be thought of as an air pump. At any specified RPM the volume of air pumped by the compressor rotor will be a definite amount. The weight of a specified volume of air will be affected by the density of the air. At 100% N1 (50,970 RPM), the compressor rotor pumps approximately 44.5 cubic feet of air per second. Thus, the weight of air pumped by the compressor rotor is determined by RPM (volume) and air density. As the air is pumped through the compressor its pressure and temperature is increased owing to compression. The compressor rotor requires a considerable amount of shaft horsepower to achieve this, and on a 'standard day' this is approximately 600 shp at 100% RPM. The gas producer turbine rotor must develop the horsepower required by the compressor rotor.

Combustion Section: The air pumped by the compressor is required

135

for combustion, internal cooling and mass flow for power development. Approximately 20 to 25% of the air is required to burn the fuel in the combustion process; the remainder is used for cooling. The hot gases of combustion are cooled by the cooling air and the cooling air is heated by the hot gases of combustion. Thus, the resulting temperature of the gases delivered to the turbine section will be within the desired limits.

The combustion section must be designed to meet the following operational requirements:
a)   provide for efficient combustion
b)   enable the engine to be started at all operational altitudes and extremes of ambient conditions
c)   control flame length, position and pattern to prevent hot spots
d)   prevent carbon formations

Turbine Section: The design of the turbine section is such as to take advantage of impact and reaction of gases passing through the gas producer and power turbines. Varying fuel flow changes the temperature of the gases passing through the turbine section and, therefore, the amount of energy in the gas stream. Varying the gas energy will result in a variation of the expansion rate of the gases as well as a change in velocity, through the turbine. Therefore, any increase in gas temperature will result in an increase in torque developed by the turbine. The torque developed by the power turbine is delivered to the helicopter rotor system.

Exhaust Section: Exhausting gases from the power turbine are directed into the exhaust collector support which provides for the exhaust flow at right angles to the engine centreline through two elliptical ducts on the top of the engine.

MORE ABOUT COMPRESSOR STALL

First of all, it must be understood that compressor stall is not a phenomenon peculiar to any one particular type of engine. It can occur on any turbine engine if conditions are right. The constant demand for more horsepower and/or lower specific fuel consumption will be met by:

a) increasing the mass airflow through the engine
b) increasing the pressure ratio of an engine
c) increasing the maximum allowable turbine inlet temperature
d) improving the efficiency of the compressor and turbine sections
    of the engine

Quick engine starts and fast accelerations are also desirable. To provide high power output with superior fuel consumption and rapid acceleration characteristics, it is necessary to operate as closely to the stall region as possible. To prevent compressor stall it will be necessary to meter fuel flow during starting and acceleration on any gas turbine engine.

Generally speaking, there has been less stall of high intensity on centrifugal-type compressors than on axial-flow types. There are several reasons for this but probably the one having the greatest bearing is the fact that the centrifugal compressors operate at much lower pressure ratios than the axial-flow types.

Compressor stall occurs in many different forms and under many different conditions. It is a mixture of many complex phenomena which are neither easy to describe nor to understand. The following is an attempt to explain compressor stall in non-technical terms.

Let us first of all review certain facts. Three things are necessary for combustion: air, fuel, and ignition. Airflow through a gas turbine is used for three things:

a) the supply of oxygen for combustion of fuel
b) the internal cooling of the engine
c) mass flow for power development

Airflow through a gas turbine engine is many times that required to burn the fuel delivered to the burner.

The ability of the compressor rotor to pump air is a function of RPM. At low RPM the rotor does not pump air as efficiently as it does at high RPM.

Compressor blades and vanes are aerofoils. Airflow will separate from an aerofoil if:

a) the flow velocity is too low
b) the angle of attack is too high

An aerofoil stalls when airflow separates from the aerofoil.

In a gas turbine engine the airflow is many times more than that required to burn the fuel. Any air not required for combustion is called cooling air. The burner uses this cooling air to control the flame length and its position so that the flame does not contact any metallic surface. The hot gases of combustion are cooled by the cooling air, and the cooling air is heated by the hot gases of combustion. This permits a satisfactory temperature distribution with an acceptable maximum temperature as the gases enter the turbine.

If an excessive amount of fuel is delivered to the burner there will be enough air to burn it; but as more air is used for combustion there will be less air left for cooling and the temperature inside the burner will be higher. This will result in a greater expansion and an increased volume of gases to exhaust. If this increased volume of gases exceeds that which can flow through the turbine, the turbine will choke.

When the turbine chokes, the pressure within the burner rises rapidly to a value which is equal to or greater than the compressor discharge pressure. Airflow from the compressor stalls if the burner pressure is equal to the compressor discharge pressure (CDP). If the burner pressure is greater than CDP, the compressor not only stalls but the gases will flow from the burner into the compressor. Either of these will result in the same thing – no airflow into the burner. This means that the oxygen available for burning is reduced, so the fire will begin to die out, causing a rapid drop in temperature, greatly reduced expansion and a greatly reduced volume of gases. Now the turbine no longer chokes and burner pressure drops to a very low value. The compressor 'sees' a very low pressure, airflow is no longer stalled and air 'surges' into the burner. This rapid movement of air moves the flame downstream through the turbine. If the velocity of gases does not exceed the burning rate of fuel, the flame will propagate back through the turbine into the burner. If there is still too much fuel flow then the cycle repeats itself at many times per second.

At the onset of a compressor stall a roughness may be produced with or without audible accompaniment of rumble. More pronounced stalls may produce noises varying in intensity from pistol shots to cannon fire and, in the case of extremely bad stalls, pulsations which cause flame, vapour or smoke to appear at the exhausts.

Engine damage due to compressor stall is not likely to occur if immediate and correct action is taken:
a)   reduce fuel flow by retarding the throttle
b)   if stall continues, shut down the engine
c)   do not open and close the throttle too quickly
d)   if turbine temperatures exceed limits, shut down the engine

ALLISON 250 SERIES – HELICOPTER ENGINE CONTROL

As we now know, the speed and exhaust gas discharge at the inlet and outlet of the gas producer turbine (N1) is modulated by controlling the rate at which fuel is burned within the combustion chamber. If fuel is increased it will increase the force of the exhaust gases against the turbine blades and cause turbine and compressor acceleration.

Thermocouple readings of the exhaust gas temperature are taken immediately after the gas producer turbine and indicate a drop in total combustion temperature. This is a measure of the energy extracted by the turbine. The aim, therefore, is to operate the engine at as near as possible to the maximum gas producer turbine entry temperature for the ultimate in power extraction, but consistent with engine reliability and life consideration. A reduction in fuel will result in a decrease of the turbine driving force and cause the engine to decelerate.

The engine also has a second turbine, the power turbine (N2), mounted in the exhaust path of the gas producer turbine and which is rotated by the force of the N1 exhaust gas. Since the N1 and N2 turbines are exhaust-gas coupled only, the output of both turbines must be controlled. This is achieved by the provision of a gas producer (N1) fuel control and a power turbine (N2) governor.

The engine output is controlled in two stages by the pilot. First, the engine must be started and increased to a speed range where the power turbine governor has control. This is accomplished by operating the twist grip throttle. The throttle has three basic positions, CUT OFF, IDLE and FULL OPEN. When it is moved from cut off to idle during engine starting, the gas producer fuel control automatically meters fuel as a function of compressor discharge air sense and N1 RPM. Engine light off, acceleration and idle stabilisation are a function of the gas producer fuel control only. Opening the throttle to full open increases N1 speed to a point where the power turbine governor superimposes its control. The power turbine governor setting is the second stage of pilot control to the engine fuel system through a N2 beep trim setting – the RPM at which the power turbine governor will govern.

One basic difference between a turbine engine and a piston engine is in the method of controlling power output. In the pison engine, power output is modulated by controlling the amount of intake air into the engine, whereas in the gas turbine it is modulated by controlling the fuel supply.

To better understand the functions of the fuel control unit and what happens when you operate the twist-grip throttle, it will be necessary to review the basic fuel requirements of the turbine engine. The graph below shows the fuel requirements plotted against engine speed at both low and high altitudes. The graph shows the amount of fuel required to maintain a constant RPM under one set of conditions, that is altitude, pressure, temperature and airspeed.

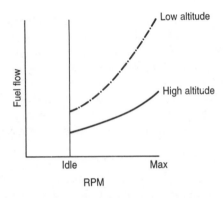

Remember that the twist-grip throttle selects only gas producer RPM. The fuel flow is modulated by a fuel control governor which regulates it to maintain the selected engine RPM.

A study of the graph 'Fuel Flow v Idle Speed' below shows why complex components inside a turbine fuel control are necessary.

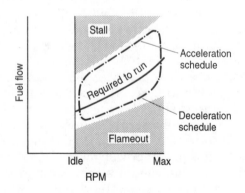

The solid line again represents the fuel flow required to run at a given RPM for one set of conditions. Fuel flow above this level will cause the engine to accelerate, and any fuel flow less than this will cause it to decelerate. The shaded areas of the graph are 'prohibited' combinations of fuel flow and RPM for these conditions. Operation in the upper shaded area will cause the compressor to stall because of the high combustion temperatures caused by the excessive amount of fuel and the resulting increase in pressure. This pressure increase raises the pressure ratio across the compressor, resulting in a lower air velocity.

For the axial flow stages of the compressor, the lower air velocities mean higher angles of attack for each blade. If the angle of attack becomes too high the blade will stall and cause a further reduction of air velocity through the engine and a reduction of RPM. The centrifugal compressor, while not as sensitive to this effect, will also stall, with similar results. A gas turbine operating in a stalled condition is literally 'spinning in', and if allowed to continue operating in this condition will destroy itself as a result of high temperature failure of the turbine blades. Operation in the lower shaded area of the graph will result in a flameout owing to the lower fuel/air ratios in the combustion chamber.

The fuel control unit operating in its normal mode prevents fuel flow/RPM combinations that are in these prohibited areas. It does this by limiting the amount of fuel delivered to the engine when an RPM change is demanded by a twist-grip throttle movement. These limits are the acceleration and deceleration schedules and are marked on the graph by dotted lines. Controlling the fuel flow to these schedules is the most critical function of the fuel control. To permit rapid acceleration of the engine the acceleration schedule must be as far above the Required to Run line as possible. During deceleration, too rich a deceleration schedule would make the engine slow to respond to an engine power demand to the fuel control unit. Too lean a schedule would result in an engine flameout.

As the prohibited areas vary with each combination of altitude, pressure, temperature and airspeed, etc., the fuel control unit must be an internally complex and critical component.

BASIC HELICOPTER FLYING CONTROLS

The basic helicopter flying controls consist of the following:

The CYCLIC PITCH CONTROL, so named because it 'feathers' the main rotor cyclically to control the attitude of the rotor disc about the longitudinal and lateral axes. Responses to movement of the cyclic are directionally the same as for aeroplanes. Here the similarity ends. Cyclic response is extremely sensitive and rapid in all flight conditions from zero airspeed to Vne.

Movement of the cyclic tilts the rotor disc, directing the lift force and giving the pilot complete attitude control. Precise rotor disc attitude control must be developed by the pilot to maintain a position over the ground or to maintain a desired airspeed in forward flight. The cyclic gives pitch and roll control in forward flight much like an aeroplane control column; however, it controls the rotor disc directly and not through elevators and ailerons. Banking turns a helicopter in forward flight just as it does an aeroplane, except that there is no adverse aileron yaw or tendency for the nose to drop in turns. Proper handling calls for smooth, precise, minute corrections – more in the nature of pressures than movements.

ANTI-TORQUE PEDALS control the collective pitch of the tail rotor blades. Usually with the pedals set at neutral the tail rotor is rigged to have positive pitch to offset torque in stabilised forward flight. Because the main rotor turns in one direction, an equal and opposite torque reaction will tend to turn the fuselage the other way. Varying power and changing airspeeds require control over the anti-torque rotor to maintain a desired heading.

Since any change of power results in a change of torque, the pedals must be co-ordinated with these power changes. Application of pedal has a tendency to affect RPM because of the increase/decrease in pitch (lift/drag) of the tail rotor blades. The power turbine governor (N2) will compensate for this and maintain a constant RPM. Pedal pressures are light and little feedback force is felt.

The COLLECTIVE PITCH LEVER is operated with the left hand and is so named because it controls the pitch of the main rotor blades collectively. It is rigged so that lifting the lever causes an increase in the main rotor pitch angle. This gives the pilot instant reaction to demands for increased or decreased lift.

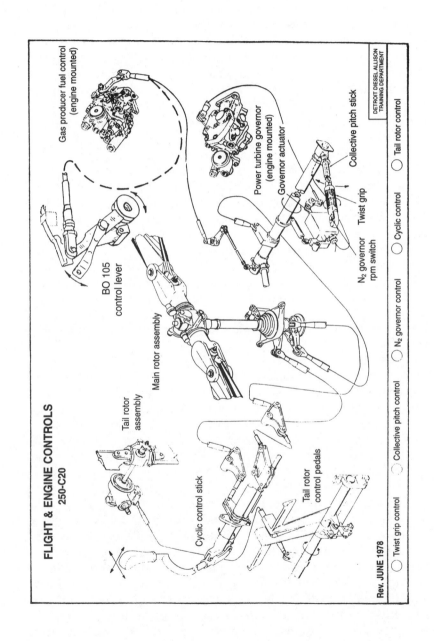

FLIGHT & ENGINE CONTROLS
250-C20

Gas producer fuel control (engine mounted)

BO 105 control lever

Power turbine governor (engine mounted)

Governor actuator

Collective pitch stick

Twist grip

N₂ governor rpm switch

Main rotor assembly

Tail rotor assembly

Cyclic control stick

Tail rotor control pedals

DETROIT DIESEL ALLISON TRAINING DEPARTMENT

Rev. JUNE 1978

◯ Twist grip control   ◯ Collective pitch control   ◯ N₂ governor control   ◯ Cyclic control   ◯ Tail rotor control

The primary function of the collective lever is altitude control; therefore it becomes the engine power demand control. The twist-grip throttle is linked to the fuel control unit and the collective lever is linked to the N2 governor in such a manner that lifting the collective increases power and lowering it decreases power while maintaining rotor RPM within operating limits. Sudden and gross movements of the lever should be avoided – corrections are of the order of smooth pressures.

The TWIST-GRIP THROTTLE has been described above, where it was pointed out that in normal powered flight operations the collective lever and throttle maintain a constant RPM through the use of an N2 governor. Thus, where it was necessary to open or close the throttle manually on a piston engine with collective pitch changes in order to maintain a given RPM, it is now automatic on a gas turbine engine and requires no throttle movement.

This now brings us to new terminology that may not be familiar to piston-engine pilots.

DROOP is the loss (or gain) of N2 RPM – this RPM change should be temporary, as the N2 governor and the fuel control need time to react to power demands. A temporary loss of RPM is referred to as transient droop and a permanent change as droop or steady state droop.

LAG is the amount of time it takes for the N2 droop condition to be corrected.

DECAY occurs when the engine can no longer deliver enough power to compensate or maintain RPM for a large collective lever increase. When this happens, the pilot is literally dragging down N2 and rotor RPM and could lose lift very rapidly due to RPM decay. In this case the collective should be lowered to regain RPM and a check should be made to see if the throttle is in the fully open position. Decay is not as readily recognisable in a gas turbine as it is in a piston engine, so the pilot must monitor the N2 tachometer and power instruments regularly to detect this condition.

Throttle operation is similar on all turbine-engined helicopters in that the direction of travel is the same – rolling the grip away from the pilot opens the throttle and rolling the grip towards the pilot closes the throttle. The full range of throttle travel is 90° from fully closed to fully open. The first 30° of travel puts the throttle on top of the flight idle mechanism stop. As this stop is passed, a slight clicking noise will be felt as the idle stop plunger springs out. This stop prevents the pilot from inadvertently shutting off the engine. Normal powered flight is accomplished with the throttle in the fully open position. The automatic function of the governor/fuel control selects the proper fuel flow to maintain a given RPM with any collective change up to maximum available power. Movement of the throttle between flight idle and full open requires smooth, slow applications to prevent excessive torque and TOT.

EFFECTS OF LOW ROTOR RPM

The rotor RPM limits shown on the tachometer are among the most important signals displayed to the pilot concerning the in-flight safety of his helicopter. The pilot should constantly check the RPM to assure that they are within allowable limits.

With piston engines, a powerplant failure or reduction of RPM is almost always immediately discernible to the pilot because of the accompanying changes in sound characteristics. Unfortunately, a turbine engine does not give as much warning of failure or loss of RPM, especially when the loss of RPM is gradual. Consequently, when flying a turbine helicopter it is important that the pilot be aware of rotor RPM decay as indicated on the tachometer.

When a pilot is concentrating on other factors connected with the flight it is important to remember to consciously continue to check rotor RPM. Excessively low RPM or power failure calls for immediate lowering of the collective lever. Even with a high inertia rotor system, power failure may result in a dangerously low rotor RPM if corrective action is delayed more than a few seconds. Remember that, as rotor RPM slows down, control power reduces, even faster than the RPM, and excessive main and tail rotor flapping will result. Excessive flapping of the main rotor may result in the rotors hitting not only the stops but other parts of the helicopter, such as the tailboom. Excessive flapping of the tail rotor may result in the loss of the tail rotor.

FLYING YOUR TURBINE HELICOPTER

The following information is not intended to provide flight instruction but just to present you with a verbal picture of the handling qualities and control application through the basic helicopter exercises.

NORMAL TAKE-OFF TO THE HOVER

A lift-off to the hover and remaining inside ground effect is the most common type of take-off and is achieved as follows:

a) Place cyclic stick neutral, collective lever fully down, throttle fully open and RPM set for flight.

b) Smoothly raise the collective lever. As the helicopter becomes light on the skids, keep straight with the pedals and level with the cyclic. Continue to raise the collective lever until the skids break contact with the ground and settle the helicopter at three to four feet (skid height) above the ground.

c) In a turbine-engined helicopter the RPM will be maintained by the governor, thus allowing you to concentrate more on outside references.

HOVERING

The control movements required to maintain a steady hover are very small (more like pressure changes), so you must try to remain relaxed if you are to avoid overcontrolling. As hovering requires fairly high power settings you must monitor your engine instruments frequently. A steady hover is achieved by using the cyclic stick to maintain a constant ground position, the collective lever to maintain the height and the pedals to hold the heading.

LANDING

Establish a steady hover at three to four feet skid height and carry out any pre-landing checks. Gently ease down the collective lever to lower the helicopter. At the same time prevent any yaw with the pedals and maintain your ground position with the cyclic. Continue until the skids touch the ground and the collective is fully down. Throughout the landing sequence you must maintain the external hover references and not be tempted to look down or at the ground just ahead of the helicopter. Once again, it is most important that you relax and use only very small control movements.

When landing and taking off the helicopter should not be allowed to remain lightly in contact with the ground for any longer than is necessary. This is because there is a slight risk that ground resonance could occur. Should this happen, you must immediately lift off to a safe hover height and allow the helicopter to settle.

DEPARTURE FROM THE HOVER TO THE CLIMB

To begin the transition a slight accelerative attitude is selected. There are several noticeable effects which then occur and, as they are all related to airspeed, they are best observed in light wind conditions.

Initial Height Loss: If the collective lever position is maintained there will be an initial height loss as the accelerative attitude is selected. This is due to tilting the rotor disc and the resulting loss of ground effect.

Flapback and Inflow Roll: Shortly after the helicopter has begun to move forward there will be a tendency for the nose to pitch up (flapback) and roll towards the advancing side (inflow roll). The combined effect can be quite marked.

Translational Lift: At about fifteen knots airspeed there is a noticeable increase in translational lift which causes the helicopter to climb. Normally this effect is accompanied by a slight buffet.

In the transition to the climb the initial height loss is prevented by the use of the collective lever and translational lift helps the helicopter to climb. The problems of flapback and inflow roll will be overcome if you select and maintain the required attitude using external visual references.

Establish a steady hover and then check that all is clear behind you. Having selected a heading reference marker well ahead, adopt a slight nose-down attitude. Maintain height with collective initially until translational lift is achieved and then set climb power. Use pedals to keep straight and cyclic to maintain best rate of climb speed.

CONSTANT ANGLE OF APPROACH TO THE HOVER

The constant angle of approach is a straight-line flight path from the point of initial descent back to the hover. The approach angle will depend on the height from which the descent is started and the distance from the hover point. Once selected, the angle is maintained using the collective lever and the groundspeed is controlled by the cyclic. The only real way of judging whether the groundspeed is correct is to scan the ground to the side of the helicopter and relate the groundspeed to the distance to the hover point – the rate of closure. An apparent fast walking pace will give the required groundspeed.

In the final part of the approach, concentrate on selecting the hover attitude and allow the helicopter to drift to a stop over the landing point. If there is any doubt that you may not be able to maintain a safe approach you must abort it and go around without hesitation.

There are two main areas of misjudgement which could prove to be hazardous unless corrected.

Excessive groundspeed in the final stages: In this situation you would be faced with a rapid transition back to the hover. This could be beyond your capability if allowed to happen in the early stages of your flight training.

Excessive rate of descent with low airspeed: Although groundspeed is the main preoccupation on the approach, airspeed cannot be totally ignored. If the airspeed is low and the rate of descent high, there is a possibility that as you apply power you could enter Vortex Ring. Generally speaking, rates of descent in excess of 500 feet per minute must be avoided at airspeeds below twenty knots.

To carry out a go-around, first select an accelerative attitude and, provided your airspeed is above twenty knots, apply climb power.

AUTOROTATION

Entry into and recovery from autorotation involves large collective lever and pedal movements. It is important, therefore, that you develop your co-ordination to carry out these movements smoothly and avoid overcontrolling.

In autorotation, rotor RPM is all important – not only does the rotor provide the thrust needed to stabilise the rate of descent, but also the inertia necessary to cushion the landing. To enter autorotation from straight and level flight, smoothly lower the collective lever to the fully down position in one continuous movement. At the same time, prevent yaw with the pedals and maintain attitude with cyclic. It is usual for the helicopter to pitch nose-down on entry. The helicopter is now in autorotation.

Select the attitude for minimum rate of descent airspeed with the cyclic and confirm that the helicopter is in balance. Maintain a good lookout while in autorotation. To recover back into the climb smoothly raise the collective lever to climb power; at the same time use pedal to prevent yaw. Maintain attitude with cyclic during the recovery – there is a tendency for the nose to pitch up as the collective is raised. Confirm balance and heading.

Turns in autorotation can have a dramatic effect on the rate of descent and rotor RPM. If the rotor RPM increase towards their upper limits, the collective lever must be raised slightly to prevent overspeeding. Remember to lower it again as soon as the risk of overspeeding has passed.

CIRCUITS

Generally speaking, most ATC units will clear helicopters to approach direct for landing or clear them on track for departure. To practise circuit flying it is therefore necessary to conform to aeroplane-type procedures, e.g. the standard training circuit. The pattern shown is chosen for its safety, its conformity to ATC procedures and its training value. Once again, lookout for other aircraft is extremely important, so you must not let your need for accuracy result in poor lookout.

The climb: The initial part of the climb is as described in transitions earlier; however, you must carry out a climbing turn at about 400 feet and using 15-20° of bank.

The crosswind leg: Roll out on to the crosswind heading and correct for any drift as necessary. Continue to climb and level off at circuit height. Use the compass and ground markers to fly accurately. The turn on to the downwind leg is made when the landing point is 45° astern of the helicopter.

The downwind leg: After completing the turn and allowing for any drift, check you are tracking parallel to the runway. Complete any Before Landing Checks. When the landing point is 45° astern, turn on to the base leg.

The base leg: Normally the airspeed is reduced along the base leg and the height adjusted so as to arrive at the turning point for final approach at a safe combination. Correct for any drift.

Final approach: Smoothly roll out of the turn so as to be lined up with your landing point. Continue straight and level until you have the sight picture for your constant angle of approach, then commence your descent.

Emergencies in the Circuit

Engine failure on climbout: In training this is normally practised above 400 feet. There is little room to manoeuvre – no more than about 30° either side of the climb heading. You must get the collective lever down immediately. Land ahead into the wind.

Engine failure crosswind: Establish normal autorotation and turn into the wind. You should find you have reasonable time to manoeuvre for the landing.

Engine failure downwind: Enter autorotation and start a turn into wind using about 40° of bank. Make sure you are 'wings' level by 300 feet AGL, regardless of heading. In winds of less than five knots it is probably easier to ignore the wind and thereby avoid a 180° turn.

Engine failure on finals: Remember, as the height reduces so does your room to manoeuvre!

It is important that in any emergency you try to carry out all, or as much as you can, of the drills and procedures relevant to the type of helicopter being flown. Some of the common errors to avoid for a safe engine-off landing are:

a) flare too late – touchdown speed too high; flare too early and you then have to depend altogether on rotor inertia

b) raising the collective lever too late – touchdown hard and fast; raise the lever too soon and the rotor RPM can decay too much before ground contact

c) touching down with a nose-up attitude could produce a severe pitch forward and result in the helicopter rolling over

d) not holding the helicopter straight with pedals for the touchdown and run-on

ENVIRONMENTAL FLYING

Increased emphasis on improving the quality of our environment requires continuous effort on the part of all pilots to minimise the effect of aircraft noise on the general public. It is important, therefore, that we as helicopter pilots demonstrate our concern by adopting flight procedures that will encourage public support for aviation.

During departure from or approach to any landing site, heliport or airfield, the climb-out or approach path should be made so as to avoid prolonged flight over noise-sensitive areas. Always plan to fly at a higher altitude rather than as low as permitted by legislation when over recreational and other noise-sensitive areas.

QUESTIONS AND ANSWERS

1. To start a gas turbine engine, the starter motor:
   A) turns the engine through one complete cycle
   B) turns the turbine only
   C) rotates the engine up to a minimum rev/min
2. The operation of the igniters is:
   A) timed to coincide with each fuel induction pulse
   B) limited to prolong their life
   C) continuous, to maintain combustion
3. If the engine compressor air is bled off for anti-icing or particle separation systems, the turbine temperature will:
   A) rise
   B) fall
   C) not alter
4. Turbine gas temperature gives a direct indication of:
   A) developed power
   B) developed torque
   C) turbine thermal stress
5. Engine fuel heaters are used to:
   A) heat the fuel intermittently to prevent fuel icing
   B) heat the fuel continuously in flight
   C) heat the fuel and prevent 'vapour locking'
6. A hung start indicates that:
   A) the engine has started normally
   B) the engine has exceeded the starting turbine temperature
   C) the engine has failed to reach self-sustaining speed
7. The power output of a free turbine is controlled by:
   A) a bypass waste gate
   B) controlling the fuel flow to the gas generator
   C) fuel flow to the free turbine
8. Indications of an engine surge are:
   A) a sharp rise in EGT and a rumbling or banging sound
   B) a sharp drop in EGT and fuel flow
   C) a sharp rise in EGT and fuel flow
9. A 'Free Turbine' gas turbine engine drives the rotor head:
   A) from a separate turbine wheel
   B) from the compressor shaft via a free wheel unit
   C) at a speed not affected by throttle setting
10. Ignition systems are energised:
    A) during the start cycle and when relight is selected
    B) during flight through precipitation only
    C) whenever fuel is being supplied to the combustion chamber

Answers

		1. C	2. B
3. A	4. C	5. A	6. C
7. B	8. A	9. B	10. A

VIBRATIONS

Some level of vibration is always present in helicopter operation. However, a pilot can always tell which are familiar and normal and those that are abnormal. Common sense dictates that you should land as soon as possible if abnormal vibrations suddenly occur.

Vibrations can originate from many sources and generally fall into three categories according to their frequency.

LOW FREQUENCY: 100–500 cycles per minute

These vibrations are usually associated with the main rotor system. They are frequency related to the rotor RPM, e.g. one vibration per revolution, (one per rev.), 2 per rev., 3 per rev., etc.

They can be felt through the controls, the airframe or a combination of both. It may be vertical, lateral or a combination of both. A lateral vibration is one that throws you from side to side. A vertical vibration is one that bounces you up and down.

Some possible causes of low frequency vibration are:-

    Main rotor blades out of track
    Damaged main rotor blades
    Main rotor dampers out of adjustment
    Worn bearings, rod ends, etc.

MEDIUM FREQUENCY: 1000–2000 cycles per minute

This type of vibration is usually associated with the tail rotor drive system. Possible causes are improper rigging, imbalance, defective tail rotor blades or defective bearings.

Medium frequency vibrations are difficult to count due to their fast rate.

HIGH FREQUENCY: 2000 cycles per minute or higher

High frequency vibrations are usually related to the engine. However, they could be associated with the tail rotor on helicopters whose tail rotor RPM is approximately equal to or greater than the engine RPM.

Causes can range from misalignment problems, worn bearings to damaged tail rotor blades. Usually, any bearings in the engine, transmission or tail rotor driveshaft that go unserviceable will result in their vibration being directly related to engine speed.

If you experience any of these vibrations you must report them immediately to your maintenance organisation. Your specific description of the vibration will greatly assist in the quick diagnosis and early rectification of the problem before it becomes serious.